8

4 types of coaching =p21
  tutoring.
  Mentoring -p74
  Consulting
  Confronting

Coaching for Commitment

Dennis C. Kinlaw

· ·

Coaching for Commitment

Interpersonal Strategies for
Obtaining Superior Performance
from Individuals and Teams

Second Edition

JOSSEY-BASS/PFEIFFER
A Wiley Imprint
www.pfeiffer.com

Published by Jossey-Bass/Pfeiffer
A Wiley Imprint
989 Market Street, San Francisco, CA 94103-1741   www.pfeiffer.com

ISBN: 0-7879-3986-2

Jossey-Bass/Pfeiffer books and products are available through most bookstores. To contact Jossey-Bass/Pfeiffer directly call our Customer Care Department within the U.S. at (800) 956-7739, outside the U.S. at (317) 572-3986 or fax (317) 572-4002.

Jossey-Bass/Pfeiffer also publishes its books in a variety of electronic formats. Some content that appears in print may not be available in electronic books.

Library of Congress Cataloging-in-Publication Data

Kinlaw, Dennis C.
    Coaching for commitment : interpersonal strategies for
obtaining superior performance from individuals and teams / Dennis C.
Kinlaw.—2nd ed.
    p.   cm.
    ISBN 0-7879-3986-2 (acid-free paper)
    1. Personnel management.   2. Employees—Training of.   3. Employee
motivation.   I. Title.
    HF5549.K498   1999
    658.3—dc21   98-40253

Printed in the United States of America

Printing   10   9   8   7   6   5

Acquiring Editor: Larry Alexander
Director of Development: Kathleen Dolan Davies
Developmental Editor: Susan Rachmeler
Senior Production Editor: Pamela Berkman
Manufacturing Supervisor: Becky Carreño
Production Editor: Carolyn Uno, Tigris Productions

For Christiana, my first and best coach.

Contents

. . . .

Preface

Coaching for Commitment: Interpersonal Strategies for Obtaining Superior Performance from Individuals and Teams is a thorough revision of my book, Coaching for Commitment: Managerial Strategies for Obtaining Superior Performance, published in 1989. A revision was necessary for several reasons.

When Coaching for Commitment: Managerial Strategies for Obtaining Superior Performance was published, the primary need at the time was to help managers and supervisors recognize coaching as one of their most important functions and to give them a tool to become successful coaches. As organizations have become more and more employee-centered and have expected more and more leadership performance from empowered employees, it has become clear that every member of an organization can and should act as a coach to others. In my work with organizations since 1989, I have consistently found that organizations that fully support innovation, risk taking, and personal initiative are characterized by innumerable instances of conversations at all levels in which individuals are clarifying goals, teaching new skills, and showing others how to improve their performance—in other words, coaching. The first reason, then, for revising Coaching for Commitment was to take into account the need to present coaching as a function that *every* employee should be expected to perform and be equipped to perform.

A second reason for revising *Coaching for Commitment* was the growth of teams and the demonstrated importance of coaching as a team leadership function. In 1991 I published a study, *Developing Superior Work Teams*, in which I identified the characteristics of superior performing teams. Superior teams were found to be characterized by leaders who were perceived and valued as good coaches. This finding has since been verified by many other studies of team formation and performance. It is fair to conclude that when we find instances in which team development and team performance have fulfilled our expectations for the better use of people and the continuous improvement of performance, we can expect to find team leaders and team members spending a good bit of their time coaching one another and coaching their teams.

A third reason for revising *Coaching for Commitment* was that my colleagues and I have conducted hundreds of coaching workshops since 1989, and we have learned a good bit more about the coaching process and the core skills required for successful coaching. Revising the book has given me the chance to include new insights about the process and skills of successful coaching.

New to This Edition

All of the material from the first edition has been thoroughly revised. In addition there is much in this edition that is completely new:

1. This edition describes coaching as a function that can and should be performed by *all persons at all levels in all organizations*, rather than a function of managers, supervisors, and other leaders. This edition, and its accompanying trainer's package, have a much wider and more general training applicability.

2. In this edition, I have simplified the coaching process models that I developed in the first edition and have treated counseling, tutoring, and mentoring as much more closely associated than I did in the first book. I no longer consider them to

be separate coaching functions, but *examples* of a single coaching process, Responding to Needs. The reason for this simplification is that all of these functions employ the same core skills and move through the same process. They differ only in content.

3. I have also made the tie between coaching and commitment more obvious in this edition than I did in the first and have shown in greater detail just how coaching is such a powerful strategy for strengthening the commitment of people to do their level best all of the time.

4. Team coaching is a topic that is completely new in this edition, and it is the subject of its own chapter. This new material on team coaching recognizes the ever-increasing importance of teams in organizations and identifies the skills required to coach teams successfully.

5. A new chapter has also been added on the topic of self-development, which gives a number of suggestions that individuals can use to improve their coaching skills. This material makes it much easier for readers to use the book as a practical tool to improve their own skills as coaches.

6. New extended examples to illustrate the process and skills of coaching have been written for this edition. These scripts support the purpose of this revised edition, which is to show that coaching is a function for all—not just a function of appointed leaders.

Targeted Readers

I have written this book with various readers in mind. First and foremost, I have written it for anyone who is interested in coaching as a performance improvement strategy. This book is a practical, "how to" guide to coaching. Next, I have written the book for leaders at any organizational level who want to make coaching a routine function that everyone is expected to perform. They will find here a description of coaching that can become the foundation for any initiative to make coaching an operating function in an organization.

I have also written this book as a resource for HRD professionals who have responsibility for developing, delivering, or marketing programs on coaching. The book will not only give consultants the conceptual basis they need to conduct coaching workshops, but it will also provide a basis for comparing the relative merit of the various training programs and books on coaching that are commercially available.

Yet another reader will find useful information in this book—the coaching consultant. For some time a demand for coaching consultants has been growing. Organizations are hiring them to coach executives and other leaders, to help them understand various aspects of their own performance, gain clarity about the way they conduct personal interactions, understand the way they solve problems, and help them clarify their own career and performance goals. HRD consultants who intend to function as professional coaches will find information and ideas that will better equip them to perform this function.

Companion Training Package for Consultants

In addition to revising this book, I have revised the companion training package for *Coaching for Commitment*, also to be published by Jossey-Bass/Pfeiffer. The training package will contain material on how to run a coaching skills training program, participant workbooks, questionnaires, and a revised set of video behavioral models that is more congruent with the realities of cultural diversity and that model not only one-to-one coaching, but team coaching as well.

Acknowledgments

This revision would not be possible but for the comments and suggestions that I have received from the many people who have read what I have written in the past about coaching, those who have used my coaching skills training programs, and those who have attended the many coaching workshops that my colleagues and I have conducted. Also, at this rather late stage in my own life, I would not have addressed the topic of coaching again if these many people had not confirmed for me over and over again the value of coaching.

I would like to thank Larry Alexander of Jossey-Bass/Pfeiffer for his interest in this revision and his many personal kindnesses that have helped me persevere to its completion during a time of considerable personal difficulty. I am particularly pleased to acknowledge the work of Susan Rachmeler, also of Jossey-Bass/Pfeiffer, who edited the draft of this manuscript. She made suggestions that resulted in significant changes to both the content and structure of this revision.

Finally, I would like to thank my wife, Stella. Once again her competence in the English language has improved the quality of my work.

Norfolk, Virginia   Dennis C. Kinlaw
November 1998

Introduction

. . . .

Sustained superior performance occurs, most of all, because people are committed to do their level best all of the time. Coaching is a proven strategy for building such commitment.

We can change organizational systems, work processes, technology, and structures. We can re-organize, re-engineer, and re-invent organizations. We can advocate stewardship for leaders, tough-mindedness for leaders, or high-mindedness for leaders. We can involve people and empower them. We can use a wide range of alternatives to improve performance, but unless we create the commitment of people who apply these alternatives to do their very best all of the time, no change in culture, systems, or leadership will work. Coaching is one major strategy for creating such commitment.

Coaching works at every level and in all organizational relationships. It works to improve the performance of individuals (including the top executives of companies), it works to improve the performance of teams, and, ultimately, it works to improve the performance of total organizations. It works because coaching creates the major factors that lead to commitment: it clarifies goals and priorities; it helps people understand what is important and what is not; it invites people to demonstrate competent influence over their performance and careers; it improves the knowledge and skills that people need to do their best; and it conveys to others just how important and appreciated they are. Coaching also helps people resolve their performance problems and challenges people to ever-higher levels of performance.

Coaching is too closely tied to the improvement of performance to imagine that it can ever become dated. Coaching has been of value for equipping people to perform and gaining their commitment to perform well for as long as people have assisted one another to do their best.

This book is about coaching and is based on my experience of more than twenty years of researching and writing about coaching and teaching the value and skills of coaching. It describes coaching as a strategy for improving performance that has special utility in today's climate of intense competitiveness for total customer satisfaction, continuous improvement, and the drive to deliver products and services 100 percent fit to use 100 percent of the time.

Coaching has always been an important managerial and supervisory function, but today *coaching is a function whose time has fully come—for everyone*. The primary reason for the increased importance and wider application of coaching is that the traditional jobs of leadership have changed. Leadership is now rarely concentrated in the jobs of manager and supervisor. Leadership has become more and more a diffused function that is exercised by everyone.

The Changing Job of Leadership

Formal leaders, under whatever name, be it executive, manager, supervisor, or team leader, are responsible for producing results. They are responsible to achieve production quotas, to develop new products, to meet sales goals, to ensure technical excellence, to solve problems in complex systems, and to complete an almost endless variety of projects. Most of all they are responsible that customers, internal or external to their organizations, are totally satisfied with the products and services they deliver.

What has become transparently obvious is that leaders may sometimes contribute *directly* to results through their technical competence, but most of their results are achieved *indirectly* through the knowledge, skills, and commitment of others.

At one time leaders were encouraged to believe that they could achieve results through people by controlling their performance. They were encouraged to believe that if they could write enough policies, make enough rules, invoke enough rewards and punishments, practice rigorous oversight and appraisal of performance, they just might plan, organize, and direct people up to a level of *satisfactory* performance.

But now no one really believes that satisfactory performance is good enough. Satisfactory performance is built on the notions of "average" and "reasonable limits." In the now and forever world of ever-increasing national and global competition, if leaders accept the goal of satisfactory performance, they inevitably accept a loss in competitiveness, a decline in market share, stagnant capital growth, and decreasing profitability.

One leadership lesson that most organizations have apparently begun to learn is that *people may do satisfactory work because they are forced to do so by a variety of controls, but they will only do superior work because they want to—that is, because they are personally committed to doing so.* The traditional control model of leadership does not work, and here are some of the reasons:

1. People can, perhaps, be managed and supervised to a satisfactory level of performance—provided there are enough controls, work is predictable, and managers or supervisors have time to give continual and direct oversight. None of these conditions, however, has existed for a long time in most organizations. Performance has more and more come under the control of the individual.

2. People have value because they can respond to unplanned events and take advantage of unexpected opportunities.

People in organizations have value over technology and systems because they take care of hundreds of problems and respond to hundreds of opportunities that no one knew would occur. Superior performance is clearly a function of such behavior.

3. People have an enormous amount of control over what they do and how much effort they put into their jobs. The majority of people in the majority of jobs could do a good deal more or a good deal less, and nobody would be the wiser—especially their immediate supervisors.

4. The only way for leaders to survive is to have people working with them who know more about what they do than do the leaders. The people who run the machines, make the tests, sell the products, deliver the services—who actually do the work—must know more about the technical requirements of their jobs than their supervisors know or can ever possibly know.

5. The response time needed to ensure customer satisfaction (one major key to an organization's success) cannot be achieved unless the people who are in most direct contact with their customers make their own decisions without recourse to the directions of higher authority.

6. People are ultimately their own bosses. It is when they view goals and standards as their own that they perform at their best.

Sustained superior performance is under the control of individual performers. All workers have control over how much energy they will put into a task. Most workers have a lot of control over which tasks they will do and how much time they will put into a task. How this discretionary energy and time is used marks the difference between the committed and the uncommitted.

We know that people are more likely to use their discretionary energy and time to pursue organizational goals when (1) they have greater clarity about these goals and their importance, (2) they can exert influence over these goals, (3) they are more competent to achieve these goals, and (4) they receive more appreciation for working tirelessly to achieve these goals.

Coaching is an alternative to leading by control. It is largely antithetical to managing performance by trying to control people. Coaching helps create people who exercise their own self-control, that is, are committed to excel in their own performance. In Chapter One, "Coaching and Building Commitment," the many ways that coaching is a leadership function particularly suited to building commitment are described.

Overview of This Book

This book contains six chapters. A brief overview of each chapter follows:

- *Chapter One: Coaching and Building Commitment.*
  Chapter One explores the meaning of commitment; discusses the visible evidence of such commitment; and shows how coaching occupies a central and dominant role for building commitment.

- *Chapter Two: Coaching Characteristics and Processes.*
  This chapter defines coaching, distinguishes informal from formal coaching, explains the four major interactions in formal coaching, and identifies the criteria for successful coaching. It also gives reasons why attempts at coaching often fail.

- *Chapter Three: Coaching Process 1: Responding to Needs.*
  A major premise of this book is that coaching must be understood and used as a process. This chapter describes the general characteristics of the coaching process and shows how all formal coaching interactions

can be managed by employing two processes: (1) Responding to Needs and (2) Initiating Alternatives. It describes in detail Coaching Process 1: Responding to Needs, along with the core skills required to use the process.

• *Chapter Four: Coaching Process 2: Initiating Alternatives.* Coaches sometimes must challenge co-workers to higher levels of performance or confront co-workers to improve performance that is below expectations. Confronting is the coaching interaction managed by Process 2. In this, important distinctions are made between confronting and criticizing. It tells why confronting problems in performance can be made unnecessarily difficult. Process 2 is described in detail and contrasted to Process 1.

• *Chapter Five: Coaching Teams.* Coaching is not only an interaction that takes place between one person and another person, but one that often takes place between one person and several other persons, especially teams. Coaching teams requires all the understanding and skills required for coaching individuals, but also requires a knowledge of the communication process that takes place in teams and the skills for managing this process. This chapter describes this special understanding and skills.

• *Chapter Six: Self-Development.* Becoming a successful coach starts with understanding the processes of coaching and the skills that one must master to use the processes. The earlier chapters describe the processes and skills of successful coaching. This chapter gives some practical suggestions for developing oneself into a successful coach.

1

Coaching and Building Commitment

A central theme of this book is that commitment is the key to superior performance and that coaching can be a powerful strategy for building commitment. It follows that learning to be a successful coach is a solid strategy for maintaining and improving the performance of individuals and teams. This chapter demonstrates just how useful coaching is for strengthening the commitment of people to do their level best all of the time. First, it will be useful to clarify just what commitment means.

The Meaning of Commitment

Developing Superior Work Teams (1991) reported a study I had made to determine the characteristics of superior teams. One dominant characteristic of superior teams was that team members felt "committed." People on superior teams we studied described themselves as

- Being focused

- Looking forward to going to work

- Caring about results and how well the team did

- Taking it quite personally when the team did not meet its goals

- Making personal sacrifices to make sure the team succeeded

- Being determined to succeed

- Never giving up

Among the many stories that I collected in my interviews of team members is the following typical example of what commitment looked like to a drafter in a design shop:

> Coming to work in our shop means *coming to work*. We meet our schedules and we expect a completed design to be just that, *complete*. We take it very personally when our customer wants to make modifications when we submit our final. It means that we didn't do a good enough job staying in touch at every step from concept to finished product.

Commitment, like motivation, is not something that we can observe directly. We infer that they exist because of what people do. We say that people are "committed" when they demonstrate over and over again their determination to do their level best and their unwillingness to give up in the face of obstacles. Committed people in organizations are tied intellectually and emotionally to the values and goals of the organization. Committed people know what they are doing, and they believe that what they are doing is important. People cannot become committed to what is vague or trivial.

Some years ago when I was consulting to a part of the old "Ma Bell" system, I had an opportunity to observe firsthand the commitment of employees to perform consistently at their very best. It was obvious that one reason these employees demonstrated such commitment was that they had such a clear understanding of what was important and stayed focused on it. What was important became obvious whenever I asked anyone what his or her job was.

Whether the employees I asked were in purchasing or installation, or members of a line crew—their answers were the same: "My job is dial tone." These employees were committed to the one overarching goal of the company. They believed that giving the customer dial tone and restoring dial tone took precedence over everything else. Dial tone was the symbol for a working phone system. They understood the goal, and they had no question but that it was of supreme importance.

Commitment follows clarity and meaning. People need to connect what they do to some larger whole. People need to know how they contribute to their organization's success.

The complaint that I often hear leaders make about the service and administrative functions in their organizations is that the people in these functions are "not committed to the bottom line" or they "don't have the big picture." These leaders are often right, but they do not often see their own responsibility for the problem.

During a consulting job that I took on with an East Coast commercial insulating firm, I was asked to resolve some of the conflicts that had arisen between the home office and the field teams. I discovered that none of the people in finance, accounting, or purchasing had ever seen firsthand their mechanics at work. They had never seen what the company did. How could they possibly have commitment to the company's real business if they had never seen it? How could they know the frustration of mechanics if they had never seen them working in hot, dirty, cramped overhead spaces insulating heat ducts? And not having seen their company's end product, how could they understand it and why should they make personal sacrifices to achieve it?

It took only a few field visits by the home office people to turn the whole problem around. When both the office people and the field people understood the goal and shared the same goal, they became committed to the same thing and all conflict disappeared.

Pushing paper can have no meaning or it can take on a meaning in itself. But better yet, it can be seen clearly as a step in fulfilling the company's mission. If we want support people to share the same commitment to the company's bottom line that those people have who are directly involved in producing products and delivering services, then we must show them what the services and products that contribute to that bottom line are. A job is only a job until it becomes a commitment, and commitment is only possible when people see the meaning in what they do.

Building Commitment Through Coaching

Figure 1.1 displays four critical conditions that contribute to the development of commitment. I have tested them many times over, and they have held up in every consulting engagement that I have had that focused on improving performance. People tend to become fully committed to do their best all of the time to the degree that they

- Are *clear* about core values and performance goals

- Have *influence* over what they do

- Have the *competencies* to perform the jobs that are expected of them

- Are *appreciated* for their performance

As I will demonstrate, coaching is a particularly powerful way to develop these conditions for individuals and teams. As I discuss each of these conditions, I will show the special contribution that successful coaching makes in creating each.

Being Clear

An accepted fundamental condition for building commitment of people in organizations is that they be clear about the organization's foundation or core values and its primary goals. Clarity about values and goals exists when people understand these values and goals

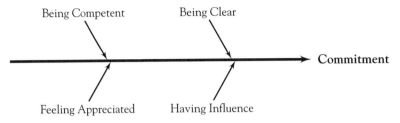

Figure 1.1. Four Critical Conditions for Building Commitment

as they work and expect that people who do so will be rewarded by the organization.

Ambivalence and confusion are the enemies of commitment. Values that are clearly communicated, adhered to, and reinforced by the behaviors of leaders give people the basis for making decisions when there are no specific rules for making such decisions. Knowing what the real values and goals of an organization are provides members a framework within which a vast variety of behaviors are possible, and it helps people resolve conflicts over priorities. When values and goals are not clear, commitment cannot be built, and performance suffers.

Coaching resolves questions about values and goals through a process of collaboration and consensus. It is easy to see the importance of clarifying goals when teams are being coached. One of the most common experiences of teams is that they "lose their way." When teams meet to resolve performance problems, make decisions, analyze performance data, set performance goals, and perform a number of other similar tasks, they often begin with high energy and determination. But as they become stuck in unprofitable conversation, go off on tangents, and lose their way, the energy drops, discouragement sets in, and members begin to feel that they are wasting their time. The team needs someone to accept responsibility to function as a coach, to help the team solve its problem, regain its effectiveness, and become committed again to its task.

I have a friend who, while he headed up an electronics research group, demonstrated his own commitment to the value of coaching as a strategy for ensuring that people understood the organization's values and goals and their importance. While he led the group, he personally held a two-to-three-hour coaching session with each new employee. He went over in great detail the history of the organization. He described the evolving nature of the organization. He talked about its culture. But he spent most of his time helping the new employee understand what the organization believed about people, about freedom in research, about mutual respect, and about accountability—in other words the core values and goals of the organization. There is no substitute for this kind of personal interchange to build clarity about core values and goals.

Core values and goals must be tested over and over again by individuals and related by them to the practical issues of work and the many decisions they make. People are helped to align themselves with the organization's core values and goals when they can test them with their leaders and colleagues in conversation, raise real problems, discuss what takes priority—when they are coached.

Issuing goals and publishing values in a work group or organization does not automatically result in their exerting practical influence over what people do. Some of the more frequent kinds of conversations that take place among peers and between workers and their appointed leaders are those in which people raise questions about what is important, what should be done first, when a job is considered complete, and how to fulfill expectations. All such questions present opportunities for coaching interactions.

Having Influence

Clarity is one condition for building commitment. Influence is another. We have all seen how people perform when they are consistently denied any say-so in their jobs and are expected to follow unquestionably the decisions of their leaders.

Leaders who deny people influence receive what they deserve. People end up doing what they are told to do—and they do it exactly! One of my favorite cartoons shows a supervisor who is wild-eyed, disheveled, and pulling his hair. Underneath the cartoon is written: "Oh my God, he did what I told him to!"

Permitting and encouraging people to exercise influence is not just an opportunity for appointed leaders. Every person in an organization is presented countless opportunities to encourage others to explore and analyze the various problems they must solve about their work and about their relationships with others. The power of self-managed teams derives from the opportunity that members have to influence the performance of these teams by the free use of their own knowledge and skills.

It takes discipline to encourage people to exert influence. Think of the many ways that we routinely inhibit people from fully expressing an idea. A friend of mine has collected what he calls "Showstopping Ways to Kill Innovation." He has recorded the kinds of comments that some of us make in response to new ideas. Here are eight of my favorites:

- "Our problem is different."

- "There are pros and cons."

- "Let's be realistic."

- "Let's study it."

- "It conflicts with policy."

- "The boss won't like it."

- "We tried that once before."

- "This is not the right time to try it."

Coaching has particular utility in extending influence to others. Every successful coaching conversation is mutual. Persons being coached are taken fully into account in successful coaching. Full use is made of what they know. Successful coaching does more. It helps people gain new knowledge and skills and discover new opportunities to exert influence over their jobs and their lives. Disciplined coaches help others identify their own needs and help them shape the ways these needs are met. Coaching sometimes helps others set their own performance expectations and their own career goals.

When you observe successful coaches in action, you probably hear them using the following kinds of phrases calculated to help others influence the outcomes of the interactions:

- "So how do you think we should go about resolving this issue?"

- "What sorts of things have you tried up to now?"

- "What would be a better way to keep our meetings on track?"

- "How about your taking a crack at simplifying the report?"

- "How do you think we should go about this performance review?"

- "What resources can you identify that might help you get up to speed on the system?"

Being Competent

A third condition that produces commitment in people to do their best all of the time is that they be competent to succeed. People do not naturally want to fail, but they will often try to avoid the tasks that they think they cannot do. If we want commitment from people, we must ensure they have the ability and willingness to succeed in their jobs. Two elements must be addressed when building competency in others: (1) We must ensure that people have the knowledge, skill, and experience to perform and (2) We must ensure that people have the confidence to perform. Coaching accomplishes both of these.

One of the most obvious results from coaching is that it is the means by which people learn much of the new knowledge and skills they need to do their best. They learn these by being coached by their peers. But coaching does more than teach new knowledge and skills. It helps others find the confidence to test what they know and to take the initiative to learn more.

Being competent results from the combination of having the knowledge and skills to perform and the confidence to use the knowledge and skills. Knowledge and skills, confidence, and performance (the key factors in being competent) are related in the following ways:

1. The more successful we are in using our knowledge and skills, the more positive feedback we are likely to receive, and positive feedback is a proven factor in improved performance.

2. As our confidence increases in demonstrating our knowledge and skills, the drive to continue to improve our knowledge and skill levels increases.

3. Increased confidence in using our knowledge and skills leads to greater freedom of mental and physical movement and increases the chance of discovering new opportunities for learning new knowledge and skills.

Here are a few of the reasons that successful coaching is such a powerful strategy for building competence. The personal, interactive nature of coaching

1. Makes it easy for people to succeed by helping them learn in small increments

2. Often provides the persons being coached with the opportunity to demonstrate and verify their new learning during the process of being coached

3. Gives people personal encouragement and support, which increases the probability of success

4. Makes it possible for people to fail safely and to learn from failure

5. Challenges people to attempt more and more difficult tasks

Coaching is the one sure way that we can find out exactly what others do not know and what they need to know. Coaching is also a way to give support and to reassure people who are taking on new tasks. Coaching facilitates, that is, "makes easy," the process of learning, because coaching is timely and focuses exactly on what each individual or team needs.

Feeling Appreciated

The fourth condition that supports commitment is appreciation. One of my untested theories is that if you want to know how people feel about their organization and their work, check the bathrooms. In one company in which I have done some consulting, the bathrooms are always immaculate. The whole place looks as though it has been scrubbed with a toothbrush. One time the "being cleaned" sign was out and the janitor was cleaning, so I took the chance to thank him and to tell him what a great job he was doing. Then I asked him, "What makes you do it? Why do you do such a great job?" He answered, "Because I know everyone appreciates it being nice."

What I later found out was that the senior leader in the building sets the example. He routinely takes special care to thank the janitor for his work. Once he prepared a letter of appreciation and took the janitor (quite by surprise) to the fourth floor to receive it from the vice president.

Over the years I have surveyed many organizations to determine employees' perceptions of several variables that we know predict an organization's performance. The variables that I have measured are employees' perceptions of clarity, fairness, responsiveness, involvement, and appreciation. The variable that employees are most likely to be least positive about is appreciation.

We all have a lot to learn about appreciation. Sometimes what people do not know about appreciation is mind-boggling. During the break in one of my seminars I heard one leader say to another participant: "Say, Dale, you mentioned during our last discussion that you make it a point to write people thank-you notes when they go out of their way or do something special. Just what sort of things do you say in those notes?"

One "tough-minded" leader said to me once: "Well, where I come from, the appreciation that you get for doing a good job is that you get to keep your job." Sounds good, but it doesn't work. Commitment to superior performance is a function of clarity, competency, influence, *and* appreciation. People work the best when they believe that what they do counts for something to someone else—especially the people with whom they work.

Among the many things that successful coaching accomplishes is that it communicates personal appreciation. Brief words of encouragement, saying "thank you," or giving concrete positive feedback about some special effort are all coaching actions. In more extended interactions that solve problems, teach some new knowledge or skill, confront unsatisfactory performance, or challenge people to attempt higher levels of performance, successful coaches use every opportunity to emphasize the strengths and accomplishments of the persons being coached. Common expressions found in extended coaching interactions include the following:

- "Thanks for putting such effort in working through this problem with me."

- "I know it wasn't easy to look at the problems you are having on the team, and I do appreciate your being so candid in talking about it."

- "I hope you will keep in mind the excellent progress you've made in implementing the new quality standard and not let this small setback cast a shadow over all the good work."

Every conversation among co-workers is potentially a coaching conversation. It is a chance to clarify goals, priorities, and standards of performance. It is a chance to reaffirm and reinforce the organization's core values. It is a chance to hear ideas and involve others in the processes of planning and problem solving. And more important than all the rest, it is a chance to say "thank you."

Key Learning Points for Chapter One

1. Commitment is a key strategy for superior organizational performance.

2. Commitment is created by

   - Being clear about goals and values
   - Having influence over one's job
   - Being competent to succeed
   - Feeling appreciated for one's contributions

3. Coaching is a major strategy for creating commitment because it uses the power of personal conversation (a) to resolve individual questions about values and goals; (b) to help people exert personal influence in solving the problems and making the decisions that affect them; (c) to teach new knowledge and skills, verify their use, and encourage people to apply what they know; and (d) to communicate to people in brief and extended interactions appreciation for their work and effort.

Reference

Kinlaw, D. *Developing Superior Work Teams*. San Francisco: Jossey-Bass/ Pfeiffer, 1991.

2

Coaching Characteristics and Processes

This book has the practical purpose of helping readers develop into successful coaches in order to assist others to become successful coaches. To fulfill this purpose, the book provides a definition of coaching so specific and concrete that it can guide us to define exactly what we need to know and what we need to be able to do to become successful coaches.

Coaching Is Everyone's Job

Coaching is not a role. It is a function. It is not just something that people with assigned leadership roles, such as managers or supervisors, do. It is a leadership function that *everyone* has the opportunity to perform and one that everyone should perform.

It is, of course, the case that people who have assigned leadership roles should be coaches, but most people in every organization have the opportunity to help their co-workers solve problems, learn new knowledge and skills, and take on more challenging tasks. They have the opportunity to encourage and give feedback to one another. Coaching does not depend on one's having a certain organizational position or title. It depends on having the desire to help others succeed and possessing the knowledge and skills that it takes to help through the process of personal conversation.

If you have ever been a member of a first-rate project, you know what coaching looks like as a distributed leadership function. It is not just the project manager or the systems manager who coaches. Coaching is a way of life. This is particularly apparent when a new person joins the project. The more experienced members tutor, mentor, counsel, and challenge the new person. The experienced members conduct a myriad of personal conversations to bring the new member "up to speed" as quickly as possible.

It is also easy to see coaching as a distributed function when we look at the best performing teams. It is characteristic of these teams that any member at any given time will be found coaching the team to use some new problem-solving technique, understand some new technology, or clarify some issue about goals and expectations.

Brief or Extended

Coaching can be a brief or an extended interaction. Coaching is taking place when we give another person a few words of encouragement. We are coaching when we say anything to anyone that helps maintain or improve that person's performance. We are coaching when we say "That was a good job." We are coaching when we say "Here is a simpler way you might try." We are coaching when we advise, "You might try contacting your client before you make that change." Coaching is taking place any time a personal and mutual interaction takes place by which performance is positively affected. Coaching is, however, often more than an informal interaction. It may be an extended conversation that has considerable structure and well-defined purposes. There are occasions, for example, when special time and effort must be made to conduct an extended conversation to teach, to respond to a co-worker's problem, or to address some performance problem. These are the occasions when coaching takes on a more extended character.

Extended Coaching Conversations

Four of the most common examples of extended coaching conversations are *counseling, mentoring, tutoring,* and *confronting.*

Counseling

Counseling includes all coaching interactions focused on solving some technical, organizational, or other problem that is blocking a person's performance. Such problems are usually presented by the person seeking help. Some typical outcomes of counseling are the following:

- Accurate descriptions of problems and their causes

- Technical and organizational insight

- Venting of strong feelings

- Changes in points of view

- Commitment to self-sufficiency

- Deeper personal insight into one's feelings and behavior

Mentoring

Mentoring includes all those coaching interactions focused on helping people understand the organizational environments in which they work or helping a person plan and take responsibility for his or her career development. Some typical outcomes of mentoring are these:

- Development of political savvy

- Sensitivity to an organization's culture

- Personal networking

- Greater proactivity in managing one's career

- Commitment to the organization's goals and values

- Sensitivity to the idiosyncrasies of senior leaders

Tutoring

Tutoring includes all those coaching interactions focused on helping people gain some new knowledge or skill. Some typical outcomes from tutoring are these:

- Increased technical competence

- Increased breadth of technical understanding

- Movement to an expert status

- Increased learning pace

- Commitment to continuous learning

Confronting

Confronting includes conversations about deficits in performance as well as ones that present opportunities for the persons coached to go to higher levels of performance and those intended to resolve some performance deficit. Some typical outcomes from confronting are these:

- Clarification of performance expectations

- Identification of performance shortfalls

- Acceptance of more difficult tasks

- Strategies to improve performance

- Commitment to continuous improvement

When we identify the four functions of coaching and then list such a large number of different outcomes for each function, we seem to suggest that coaching is a very complex strategy to maintain or improve performance. It should follow, then, that leaders must undertake the arduous task of learning different processes and skills for performing each function. However, my studies indicate just the opposite.

All four functions share so much in common that it is unnecessary and pointless for us to learn separately how to counsel, how to mentor, how to tutor, and how to confront. All of these coaching examples share so much in common that we can learn to be successful coaches by concentrating on the processes or sequences that give shape to successful coaching. Two such processes, which apply to most coaching conversations, are covered below.

Attributes of All Coaching Interactions

All coaching interactions share at least two common attributes:

1. They are conversations of personal discovery
2. They focus on performance or performance-related topics

Personal Discovery

Coaching consists of conversations that are specific to the needs and interests of the persons coached. Coaching is shaped by discovering what the other person does know and does not understand. It is shaped by responding to specific problems and questions. For example, coaching people to learn new knowledge and skills is a highly interactive process of give-and-take in which the persons coached set the agenda by their questions and expressed needs. Classroom training, on the other hand, proceeds by setting objectives that apply to all participants—whether or not they are appropriate to each individual.

Focus on Performance

Coaching conversations focus on performance. Performance, however, should not be understood in some restrictive sense as applying only to knowledge, skills, tasks, and objectives. It is the whole person who performs. Coaching includes any topic that concerns a person who performs. The underlying assumption of coaching is that all of us can help one another. This help may be assisting others: to solve a problem or gain some new insight (counseling), to learn the "unwritten" rules of an organization or gain political savvy (mentoring), to learn some new knowledge or skill (tutoring), or to correct performance deficits or rise to higher levels of achievement (challenging). In all cases, the ultimate goal is to help others reach new levels of personal commitment for sustained, superior performance.

Leaders sometimes ask me, "Don't you think there are some topics or problems that we should not discuss with employees?" My answer is, "Name one." Of course we will not always be able to help others resolve all of their problems. We are not all therapists, but we can all be coaches. We cannot solve substance abuse, tobacco addiction, marital conflict, and such problems. It is not appropriate that we try. But it is always appropriate for us to show people where to find help—regardless of the nature of a problem.

Criteria for Successful Coaching

All coaching is a *personal conversation* of discovery that, in some way, is *focused on performance*. But even when coaching has these two characteristics, it may not be successful. How can we know that a coaching conversation is successful? My investigations suggest the following criteria. Successful coaching

1. Results in positive performance change and new or renewed *commitment* to

   • Self-sufficiency
   • The organization's goals and values
   • Continuous learning
   • Continuous improved achievement

2. Results in achievement or maintenance of positive work relationships

3. Is a mutual interaction

4. Communicates respect

5. Is problem focused

6. Is change oriented

7. Follows an identifiable sequence or flow and requires the use of specific communication skills

Results in Positive Performance Change and Commitment

Successful coaching always results in at least one positive change in performance. Exactly what the change is depends on the subject of the coaching conversation. Counseling produces the resolution of problems affecting performance. Mentoring provides understanding of a company's culture and assists people in making their career decisions. Tutoring results in learning new knowledge or skills. Confronting presents people with the chance to take advantage of their full potential or to fix some specific performance shortfall. But successful coaching does more than produce some immediate result. Successful coaching achieves the long-term result of new or renewed commitment to sustained, superior performance and continuous improvement.

Results in Achieving or Maintaining Positive Work Relationships

Coaching is successful only when it also results in achieving or maintaining positive relationships with the persons being coached. Positive relationships do not mean social intimacy. Positive relationships mean that the coaches achieve and maintain a level of comfort with the persons coached that permits the coach and coached to stay focused on the job to be done—without spending time trying to work around one another.

Is a Mutual Interaction

All coaching conversations are mutual, that is, fully interactive and characterized by the full participation of the person being coached. They are reciprocal and balanced. Successful coaching is not a didactic process—one in which the coach talks and the other persons listen. It is always a process of mutual exploration and discovery.

Both the coach and the person being coached contribute special knowledge, experience, and insights to the coaching conversation. The persons being coached bring their own personal needs, perceptions, expectations, and firsthand knowledge of their jobs. The persons doing the work are the ones who know most about how best to do the work. Coaches may bring experience, political savvy, broad technical understanding, and clarity about performance expectations. Coaching is a process designed to make the most of what *both* know. The leader's coaching task is to ensure that both sets of information are used.

Communicates Respect

Respect is what others experience because of what we do as coaches. Respect results when we encourage co-workers to give opinions, to provide data, to discuss frankly what they do not understand, and to offer objections to what we might say.

It is easy for us to become confused about respect. People who have attended my coaching workshops sometimes ask me, "How am I supposed to treat people when they aren't worthy of respect?" Or they ask, "How am I supposed to respond to something that I know is just an excuse?" or "How can I pretend that people are doing a good job when I know they aren't?"

These questions suggest a common confusion about respect. We think of respect as something that people earn or we think of it as treatment we give to those who deserve it. Respect during a coaching conversation is a characteristic that helps the conversation work. When it is present, the coaching conversation has a good chance of being successful. When it is not present, the coaching conversation will inevitably fail.

When we coach, we must never lose sight of what we are trying to achieve—positive change and commitment to sustained, superior performance. In a coaching conversation it serves no good purpose to stimulate resistance, to foster resentment, or to block the sharing of information—all of which are likely to occur when a coach does not communicate respect.

Think about what happens when we do not feel respected by another person in a conversation. This occurs when the other person does not listen, interrupts us, discounts the value of our ideas, and so on. What is going on when others behave this way is that they are not encouraging us to participate fully in the mutual development of information.

On the other hand, we do feel respected when the other person listens, asks questions, and takes our input seriously. We feel respected to the degree that we have been encouraged to contribute information and ideas.

Is Problem Focused

The job of designated leaders like managers and supervisors is to manage performance. But everyone who works with other people— the great majority of us—shares this responsibility. A performance "problem" may be a deficit of some kind or it may represent a step up to an even more difficult challenge. A problem is not necessarily something negative. It describes only the difference between what "is" and what is "desired to be." It may represent the difference between performing "very well" at one level of responsibility and performing "well" at a higher responsibility.

Successful coaches stay focused on what can be objectively described—plans, actions, events, data, and the like. *Their objective is always to fix performance, not to fix people.*

Attitudes, feelings, and general characteristics are not performance. They are guesses about what is going on with a person.

Saying something like "You are not a team player" to a person is describing a general characteristic that must be translated into specific behaviors before it can be profitably discussed. Telling another person "You are very willing and always show a good attitude" communicates only that the person is positively regarded. Advising another person that "The farther up the ladder you go, the more you are expected to talk optimistically about the company" may sound like good advice, but it is too general for the person to use in any practical way. When we coach we must make every attempt to use terms and phrases that are behaviorally specific and related directly to the objectives of the conversation.

Is Change Oriented

We learn from the past, but we cannot alter it. Successful coaches point people to what can be improved, modified, and changed. We should always approach a coaching session with the expectation that performance and commitment will be better because of the session. The past should be used only to help others understand how to improve the future.

We must avoid any behavior that encourages others to become defensive, to feel guilty, or to lose confidence. The purpose of coaching is not to help people feel better or to despair over their competencies. The purpose is to find special ways for people to be superior performers. For example, when a manager or supervisor asks a co-worker, "Why have you been late so often?," it is an invitation for the co-worker to become defensive and to find excuses. "What do you think you might do to get to work on time" is an invitation to make a change. "You really disappointed me by not turning that report in on time" encourages a co-worker to feel guilty and become apologetic. "I need that report, and I would like to know when you can have it ready" reminds a co-worker that there is a tomorrow and that change is possible. "You're still making the same mistakes that we covered last time" focuses a person on failure. "Let's see what you've picked up on since our last conversation, and then go on to where you think you still need help" focuses the person on success.

Follows a Process and Uses Specific Communication Skills

Successful coaching follows an identifiable sequence or flow and requires the use of specific communication skills. Coaching emphasizes the interpersonal dimension of leadership. Leaders stipulate, monitor, review, and assess results through a variety of formal and informal problem-solving interactions with others. It is the quality and success of these interactions that leaders influence most directly—much more so than they directly control performance.

If we mean to control the topics and content of a coaching conversation, then this is all but impossible because these conversations are with other people who also have some need to control. However, if we think of controlling as creating a *process* or flow that is satisfying to the persons being coached—one in which they willingly participate—then we can exert significant control in coaching. A full description of the characteristics of a coaching process will be presented in Chapter Three.

Successful coaches are disciplined. They do not do or say whatever comes to mind. They do and say what furthers the process of coaching toward successful outcomes. Undisciplined conversations, in contrast to coaching conversations, do not follow specific stages and do not employ the intentional use of specific communication skills. A common example of our lack of discipline is the ease with which we start solving problems before we have developed sufficient information to even understand the problem. Another example is our tendency to give information about some action or procedure that is not helpful because the information is irrelevant to the other person's needs.

Desired outcomes occur most consistently in coaching when we concentrate on developing a satisfying *process*, rather than when we concentrate on controlling the *content* of the coaching conversation. Being an effective coach depends, then, on one's ability to create and manage the process of a coaching conversation. The idea that coaching is a process and that coaching successfully requires that we manage the process is a central idea of this book, and I will return to it many times.

The Two Processes of Coaching

Coaching in all of its functions takes two generic shapes and follows two generic processes. I have chosen to call the first Process 1: Responding to Needs and the second Process 2: Initiating Alternatives. These two titles are somewhat arbitrary, but they provide a practical way of distinguishing and remembering the two processes.

Process 1: Responding to Needs

Counseling, mentoring, and tutoring are coaching conversations that follow the same process: Responding to Needs. This process starts with the need to solve a problem, learn something more about organizational realities, or learn new knowledge or skills. It may be initiated by a person asking for help or it can be initiated by someone who perceives that another person might need some help.

The needs that are appropriate opportunities for coaching always bear in some way on performance. These needs may be ones that must be responded to immediately, for example, help with some current project, clarification about conflicting priorities, or help with a personal crisis. Or these needs may concern distant career goals, future professional experiences, or long-term learning projects.

Process 2: Initiating Alternatives

The coaching conversation managed by this process is confrontation, which differs markedly from those conversations that are the subjects of Process 1. Coaching conversations that confront are always initiated by a coach who wants to help improve another person's performance. Coaches may perceive that a co-worker could move to more difficult job challenges and take the initiative to present the co-worker with the possibility. Coaches may also perceive some shortfall in a co-worker's performance and take it upon themselves to confront the co-worker about the problem.

Successful Coaching: A Working Definition

All successful coaching conversations are pointed toward improving performance and ensuring a commitment to sustained superior performance. As I have already shown, these results can only be achieved through the mutual development of information. Another outcome of successful coaching is the maintenance or improvement of a positive relationship between leaders and co-workers. Besides bearing directly on achieving good performance results, information is the basis for all positive relationships. Trust, candor, and cooperation all depend on both coaches and the persons coached sharing a common body of information.

The two coaching processes of Responding to Needs and Initiating Alternatives provide us with a simple framework for understanding coaching and for equipping ourselves to become better coaches. The most effective and efficient way for us to improve our coaching practices is to learn how to manage the two generic processes. These processes are discussed in detail later in this book.

We know that there are some specific skills that are required for developing and using the processes of successful coaching. These skills are covered in the chapters on the coaching processes. Many of these core skills serve to develop information, which is always a critical part of successful coaching.

I propose the following definition of coaching: *Successful coaching is a mutual conversation that follows a predictable process and leads to superior performance, commitment to sustained improvement, and positive relationships.*

Why Some Coaching Fails

Before proceeding to the next chapters, in which the processes and skills of coaching are described, let's clear up a few misconceptions that people often have about coaching.

Lack of a Process Model

In conducting seminars on coaching, I routinely hear a large number of "what if" questions, such as the following:

- "What if the other person goes off on a bunch of tangents and doesn't want to discuss what I want to talk about?"

- "What if I have a co-worker who is perfectly satisfied in his or her job and doesn't want to go any higher?"

- "What if the other person doesn't ever accept the fact that there is a problem?"

- "What if the person I am trying to coach doesn't want to tell me why he or she is not focusing on the job?"

At first glance, these questions seem to be raising a variety of issues about coaching. However, when I have explored them in some depth with the people raising them, I always find the same underlying issue. People often have no way to analyze systematically what works and what does not work in coaching because they have no baseline or model against which they can compare what they do. Before we begin to learn that successful coaching follows a sequential process model (such as the two I am proposing), we think of our coaching conversations as random inputs from ourselves and the people we are trying to coach. Sometimes these conversations work and sometimes they do not, but, in the end, we neither know why they worked or why they did not work.

Coaching that does not follow a proven process may sometimes succeed, but it will more often fail. Until we discipline ourselves to employ a specific model for coaching, we will always be stuck with an endless number of "What if?" questions. Until we know exactly what we are doing in a coaching interaction, that is, working from a well-defined process, we can never answer our "What if?" questions. Coaching conversations that have a random shape produce random results. Coaching does not fail, but people who do not know and use a proven process of coaching will often fail.

Lack of Responsibility

In all the years that I have been teaching people to coach, I have never once had participants offer an example or anecdote that described what *they* did wrong in a coaching interaction. When they talk about the difficulties that they have faced in coaching, I have been left with the feeling that they believe it was always all the other person's fault. As I listen to their stories, I develop a recurring image in my mind of a person being coached with no coach present.

Coaching is an interaction. What we do stimulates alternative reactions in the persons being coached. What other persons do in a coaching interaction creates the necessity to respond, and we must choose among an open set of alternatives in reacting. Whether we admit it or not, we influence the outcomes of every coaching session—and we influence these outcomes for better or worse. Coaching does not fail because the people being coached are poorly endowed or poorly motivated. It fails because of poorly trained and poorly disciplined coaches.

Key Learning Points for Chapter Two

1. Extended coaching conversations are typically of four kinds:

   - Counseling
   - Mentoring
   - Tutoring
   - Confronting

2. The criteria for successful coaching are that it

- Results in positive performance change and new or renewed *commitment* to

  - Self-sufficiency
  - The organization's goals and values
  - Continuous learning
  - Continuous improved achievement

- Results in achievement or maintenance of positive work relationships
- Is a mutual interaction
- Communicates respect
- Is problem focused
- Is change oriented
- Follows an identifiable sequence or flow
- Requires the use of specific communication skills

3. We are often not successful in coaching because we

- Do not follow a process model
- Tend to fault the persons being coached for our performance as coaches, rather than accept personal responsibility for the outcomes of our coaching conversations

Coaching Process 1: Responding to Needs

Coaching Process 1: Responding to Needs describes all those extended coaching interactions that resolve problems, result in new understandings of an organization's culture, or result in people acquiring new knowledge or skills. These conversations are sometimes initiated by the person who wants to give help (the coach) and at other times by the persons who need help, that is, the persons being coached. These conversations may differ in content, but they follow the same process.

General Characteristics of Process 1

A fundamental assumption of this book is that coaching is most likely to be successful, that is, produce commitment to improved performance and maintain positive relationships, when coaches use the interactive processes described here. Successful coaching processes are logically and psychologically satisfying to those coached and characterized by interdependent stages.

Logically Satisfying

A general way of describing the process is that it is a conversation that follows a flow that is logically satisfying for the person being coached. It is because the process is satisfying that it works. The idea of *satisfaction* gives us a new and useful way to think about our coaching conversations. It means that we must be sufficiently disciplined to create a process that naturally meets the needs of the people being coached, that is, one in which they feel comfortable and one they value.

Over the years I have had the opportunity to observe many people as they conducted coaching conversations. I have found that most people concentrate directly on the results that they want to achieve rather than creating a conversation by which these results can be achieved. They will focus on the issue that the other person presents and try to identify solutions, or they will concentrate on what they think the other person needs. In other words, they will concentrate on the *content* of the coaching interaction rather than the *process* of that interaction.

Successful coaching always produces useful results. These results, however, are the final outcomes. To achieve these final outcomes, the conversation itself must meet the needs of the person being coached.

Think of it this way. In a counseling conversation the other person may want to resolve some misunderstanding that has developed with a co-worker. In a mentoring conversation the coach may want to ensure that the other person has a clear understanding of some senior executive's priorities. But reaching these results depends on the other person's willingness to cooperate. The coach's job is to create this willingness to cooperate (or at least not to damage it) during the coaching conversation. Cooperation becomes the sufficient condition for achieving the final results of coaching. It is cooperation in the coaching conversation that fosters the other person's desire to find the best solutions *with* the coach. Coaching conversations are logically satisfying when the persons being coached

- Perceive the coach as being concrete and descriptive

- Experience an orderly progression from one point to the next

Concrete and Descriptive

None of us feels satisfied in conversations or relationships if we sense that we are being subjected to the whims and biases of another person. Coaching conversations will not be positive experiences for people if they are based largely on the coach's subjective perceptions and opinions or the coach's inferences about the other person's attitudes or motives.

Concreteness helps create objectivity, which is a highly desirable goal. No one can achieve it. It is, however, of critical importance that coaches strive to come as close to the goal as possible. Coaching interactions are destroyed whenever the person being coached feels that he or she is being treated in an arbitrary or high-handed manner.

Being concrete and being descriptive are related coaching skills. We are being *concrete* when we reason from verifiable information. We are being *descriptive* when we provide as much verifiable information as possible.

We can think of being concrete in a coaching interaction as creating a reference point that both the coach and the person being coached can agree exists, that both understand, and that both can use in making decisions during the coaching interaction. Coaching is most concrete when we create reference points such as the following:

- Performance expectations that are finite, concrete, and achievable

- Reliable measures of productivity and quality

- Verifiable selection and promotion criteria

- Specific skills that need to be mastered

- Specific causes for a problem

- Accurate problem definition

The following are examples of less concrete and more concrete inputs that a coach might make during a coaching conversation:

Less concrete: "So, the root of the problem is that your contract monitor makes unrealistic and arbitrary demands on you."

More concrete: "So, the root of the problem is that your contract monitor is asking for services that go beyond what our contract authorizes."

Less concrete: "The key to getting ahead in this organization is to be a team player."

More concrete: "There are two keys to getting ahead in this organization: first, be immediately responsive to any requests for help that come from your co-workers and, second, never make others look foolish or incompetent in front of their peers."

Less concrete: "It seems as if we are back to square one. It doesn't look as though your technical writing course has solved the problem."

More concrete: "Let's go over this last paper, section by section, and compare each section to the guidelines that you learned in your technical writing course."

Less concrete: "Your sense is that we never established what I expected about the report."

More concrete: "The problem seems to be that you were unclear about the contents of the report and the date I wanted you to submit it."

Being descriptive refers to the amount of verifiable information that we put into a coaching conversation. Being descriptive, like being concrete, increases the possibility of being objective.

Here are a few examples to illustrate what becoming more descriptive sounds like:

Less descriptive: So, the root of the problem is that your contract monitor makes unrealistic and arbitrary demands on you.

More descriptive: There seem to be at least two ways that your customer is exceeding authorizations in the contract: first by asking for extra progress reports and second by asking for more meetings than the travel budget will support.

Less descriptive: The key to getting ahead in this organization is to be a team player.

More descriptive: To get ahead, it is imperative during your first two or three years in the company to establish yourself as a responsive, cooperative, helpful person. There are several ways to do this: first, never turn down your peers when they ask for help; second, anticipate the needs of others and offer to help whenever you have the chance; third, never miss a deadline; and fourth, make sure you know exactly what your supervisor's priorities are.

Less descriptive: It seems as if we are back to square one. It doesn't look as though your technical writing course has solved the problem.

More descriptive: Let's review the recommended guidelines for technical papers that you learned in the course. Then I would like you to compare each section of your paper with these guidelines to see where you can find opportunities for improvement. I will then review each section, and the two of us together will identify the changes to make.

Less descriptive: Your sense is that we never established what I expected about the report.

More descriptive: We only had one meeting to discuss the report and the due date. I walked away with one understanding and you with another. In the future, we need to take a minute at the end of our conversations to ensure that we have a common understanding on key points.

Orderly Progression

Coaching conversations are most likely to be satisfying if they follow an orderly sequence. Tutoring conversations proceed best if what is to be learned is made clear and then each learning step is identified. Problems in a counseling session are best resolved if all the relevant information about the general problem is explored first, then the general problem is refined to a specific one, and finally the contributing causes for the problem are listed. Orderly progression presupposes that coaches have in mind some process that they are following. Successful coaches ensure that the persons being coached are clear about what the conversation is trying to accomplish. They ensure that all the information required to help the persons being coached to act responsibly is developed. If more than one topic comes up, coaches help arrange the topics so they can be considered sequentially. If the persons being coached seem to go off on tangents and begin to introduce issues that are not related to the purposes of the conversation, coaches will help them understand what they are doing and decide just what is important at the moment to them. Here are some types of statements that successful coaches might make during their coaching conversations to ensure an orderly progression:

- "You have mentioned a number of problems that you are having getting the project back on schedule. Which one should we focus on first?"

- "I think before we jump ahead and look at how these two pieces of software work together, it would be best to have a working knowledge of how they work independently."

- "It might be more use to you if we looked at all the jobs that are vacant right now in purchasing before you decide to apply for the analyst job."

- "I've given you my sense of what needs to be fixed. How do you see things?"

Psychologically Satisfying

Coaching conversations are not only logically satisfying, but they are also psychologically satisfying. They are psychologically satisfying when people

- Perceive that they can seriously influence the outcomes of the conversation

- Believe that their emotions are acknowledged and understood

- Have a sense of completeness or closure at the end of the conversation

Extending Influence

Extending influence was discussed in Chapter One as a strategy for building people's commitment. In each coaching conversation, coaches encourage others to be influential by, first of all, making the conversation truly mutual. The degree to which influence is experienced is decided by the way questions such as the following are answered.

- Did the persons being coached participate fully in deciding the nature of the problem?

- Were the persons being coached involved in researching their own options?

- Did the persons being coached help determine their learning goals and speed of instruction?

- Did the point of view of the persons being coached on performance opportunities or problems receive full consideration?

It is the interactive quality of a coaching conversation that ensures that others influence the process and outcomes of coaching. Coaches initiate interaction by behaviors that stimulate others to respond; that is, they ask questions. Coaches support the continuation of interaction by responding to what others communicate; that is, they acknowledge and they make reflecting responses.

Emotions Are Accepted and Understood

When we discuss anything that is important to us, we have feelings about what we are discussing. We soon give up trying to discuss a topic with others when they do not recognize and accept what we feel. We find interactions with others fully satisfying only when we come to believe that they accept what we are feeling and have some sense of what the feeling means. Inept coaches are soon found out because they say things such as, "Don't get so angry," "This is no reason for you to be upset," or "If you can't stop talking about how disappointed you are, we'll never figure out what to do." Successful coaches are quick to acknowledge how others feel and give others the chance to talk about how they feel.

A Sense of Closure

Not all extended coaching conversations accomplish all that is needed. Additional sessions may be required for persons coached to finish acquiring a set of skills, to find out some more information, or to finish exploring the causes for some problem. But all fully successful coaching conversations create a sense of closure or completeness. If closure is not achieved at the end of a coaching conversation, the persons being coached will feel that nothing has been accomplished, that the conversation has been irrelevant, or that they were not given an opportunity to communicate their concerns.

In every tutoring session, for example, closure occurs when people feel that they have learned something concrete. In a session that confronts unsatisfactory performance, the person being coached has a sense of closure if the problem has been accurately identified and progress has been made to resolve it.

The first two necessary attributes for successful coaching processes are that they satisfy certain logical and psychological needs of people being coached. To become successful coaches, we must learn how to create satisfying processes with the persons we coach in order to maximize their willingness to cooperate.

Interdependent Stages

A third characteristic of successful coaching processes is that they proceed through certain identifiable stages, each with its own goals. The goals of one stage must typically be met before the conversation can move to the next stage.

Coaching Process 1: Responding to Needs (shown in Exhibit 3.1) has three stages: *involving*, *developing*, and *resolving*. These stages flow into one another. As coaches use the process, they will sometimes find themselves accomplishing some of the goals in Stage I as they are moving to Stage II. In actual practice, they will find themselves moving back and forth between stages and recycling back through the whole process. Often the real issue only surfaces just as we think a counseling session is ending. Or we find that we thought we had covered a learning point in a tutoring session only to find as we try to end the session that the other person has missed the point. Figure 3.1 illustrates the cyclical and iterative nature of most extended coaching conversations.

Process Skills

Two kinds of skills are shown in Exhibit 3.1. First is a set of general skills relevant to any stage of the process that successful coaches use throughout their coaching conversations. They are displayed

Exhibit 3.1. Coaching Process 1: Responding to Needs

Goals	Stage-Specific Skills	General Skills (typically useful at all stages)
Process Stage I: Involving		
Clear expectations	*Clarifying:* Establishing the objectives	*Attending:* Using nonverbal behavior to communicate and listening without evaluating
Comfort		
Trust		*Acknowledging:* Verbal and nonverbal indications of being involved in the conversation
		Probing: Asking questions and directing
		Reflecting: Stating in one's own words what the other person has said or is feeling
		Indicating respect: Not using behaviors that ridicule, generalize, or judge
		Self-disclosure: Indicating that one has had a similar experience
		Immediacy: Drawing attention to what is happening in the conversation
		Summarizing: Pausing in the conversation to summarize key points

Exhibit 3.1. *continued*

Goals	Stage-Specific Skills	General Skills (typically useful at all stages)
Process Stage II: Developing		
Information	*Resourcing:* Providing information, advice, instruction, demonstration, or referral	Attending
Insight		Acknowledging
Problem definition/ causes		Probing
		Reflecting
	Confirming: Ensuring that results of conversation are mutually understood	Indicating respect
Learning		Self-disclosure
		Immediacy
		Summarizing
Process Stage III: Resolving		
Resolution	*Reviewing:* Going over key points of session to ensure common understanding	Attending
Next steps		Acknowledging
Commitment		Probing
		Reflecting
Positive relationship	*Planning:* Building strategies and agreeing on next steps	Indicating respect
Closure		Self-disclosure
		Immediacy
	Affirming: Commenting on a person's strengths and positive aspects	Summarizing

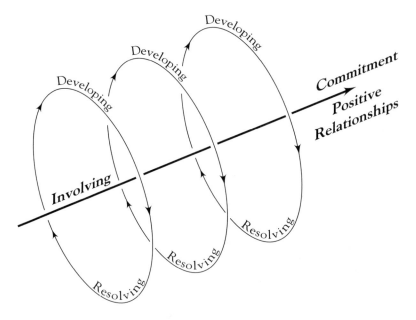

Figure 3.1. The Cyclical Nature of Coaching

in the right-hand column, which runs the length of the coaching process model.

The skills in the second set are dependent on the stage of the process and have special relevance to the stage in which they are noted. The competent coach is primarily concerned with creating a process that moves from Stage I to Stage II to Stage III. The skills support the movement of the process.

Both Coaching Process 1: Responding to Needs and Coaching Process 2: Initiating Alternatives (covered in Chapter Four) are graphic descriptions of the two principal coaching processes that underlie most extended coaching interactions. They both depict process models that have been derived from the observation of hundreds of successful coaching conversations in a controlled laboratory setting, in hundreds of coaching workshops, and in real life. As such, they provide us with a guide that we can use with confidence to achieve practical results and adapt to each situation in which we undertake the various coaching functions of counseling, mentoring, and tutoring.

General Skills

The general skills in Process I apply to the entire process and have general utility throughout the process. These skills are attending, acknowledging, probing, reflecting, indicating respect, self-disclosure, immediacy, and summarizing.

Attending

Attending has two aspects:

- Coaches have the physical discipline to convey to others that they are being listened to

- Coaches have the mental discipline to listen to understand

Attending includes all those behaviors that communicate to others that we are listening, including nonverbal behaviors, such as not doing anything that distracts, facing the other person, keeping an open posture, and being appropriately animated.

. . . .

One of the managers with whom I worked some years back made a lasting impression on me about the importance of attending. This manager apparently had a great preoccupation with time. Whenever he asked me into his office to counsel, mentor, or tutor me, he invariably had me sit underneath a clock. Throughout the entire conversation his head would bob up and down between the clock above me and my face. It was a singularly distracting behavior. I always felt that I was an imposition and that whatever time I took up was too much. I was always torn between wanting to give important information and being afraid that I was taking up too much time by giving the information.

. . . .

The physical aspects of attending communicate to others in a direct and unambiguous way that we are listening. Attending behaviors encourage others to communicate and facilitate our reaching the Stage I goals of comfort and trust.

A second aspect of attending is to listen to understand. What this means in practice is that we must listen without evaluating what the other persons are communicating—listen without immediately taking sides or deciding that another person's statement is true or false, right or wrong. It is the skill of focusing on what the person being coached is saying and trying to discover the meaning. We listen without evaluating by

- Making sure that we understand a question before we try to answer it

- Not forcing a problem into our own frame of reference and mind-set

- Not deciding whether what the other person has said is right or wrong

All of us probably have had experiences during a conversation with someone who intended to help and who doubtlessly thought he or she was helping, such as the following:

- The person responded to a question by answering another question that you did not ask.

- The person treated some failure as though you did not know how to perform the job and spent time tutoring you on some procedure that you really understood. You were never able to explain that your problem was lack of resources or some other environmental block.

- The person asked for your opinion about an issue, but when you gave it, he or she spent the next ten minutes telling you why it was a stupid opinion.

Successful coaches listen during the early stages of a conversation in order to understand, without evaluating. The danger is that we can quickly create blocks to the free and easy development of a mutual interaction by communicating too quickly that we do not agree with something.

Acknowledging

Acknowledging includes all those brief verbal responses that communicate to another person that we are fully present and that we are involved in a conversation. Some examples are

- Brief verbal statements such as "uh huh," "mmmm," "I see," "O.K.," "yes," "right," or "I understand"

- Assurances such as "Yes, I follow that," "I can see that," or "I know how you felt"

- Comments such as "So, that's how it happened," "I just made the connection you've been driving at"

Acknowledging behavior stimulates others to continue and to expand on what they are saying. It furthers the gathering of information, forcing us to listen and not to interrupt. It keeps us away from evaluative responses and other mistakes.

Probing

Probing refers to those behaviors that request or direct. During a coaching session, coaches may request information by asking a question, or they may politely ask the other person to give information.

There is no practical difference in the results between a directive probe such as, "Please tell me what happened," and a questioning probe such as, "Could you tell me what happened?" Both stimulate the gathering of information.

Closed probes encourage "yes" or "no" responses or short responses with single item content. Some examples of closed probes are as follows:

closed

- "How much money is left in the budget?"

- "Which directive did you apply in this case?"

- "Tell me the most important new skill that you want to learn."

- "Have you discussed this with your lead engineer?"

Open probes encourage elaboration. Some examples follow:

open

- "Tell me how you are getting on with the project."

- "Tell me how you decided which of the directives applied."

- "What are your general career expectations at this point?"

The purpose of all probes is to develop information. The use of open probes is like going fishing with a net. You catch a number of fish. Closed probes are like fishing with a hook. You are trying to catch one fish at a time. If you are at a point in a coaching conversation at which you are trying to gather as much information from the persons being coached as possible, then open probes typically help you to do just that. But if you are focusing on some specific issue, trying to eliminate alternatives, or testing for concurrence, then closed probes are useful.

Closed probes may not always be responded to as closed probes. The question, "Do you have enough resources to complete the project?" has the form of a closed probe, but the person would most likely give an extensive description of what resources were still needed to finish the project. We cannot predict how others will respond to any probe. So long as the coach is successful in involving others and developing the information that is required, it does not matter what sort of probes he or she uses.

A note of caution: As I have watched people conducting coaching conversations, I have observed their strong bias for closed probes. Most of us will typically use two to three times as many closed probes in a coaching conversation as open probes. If we are not careful, our coaching conversations will look similar to an interrogation by a lawyer or a diagnostic interview by a doctor.

When closed probes are strung together, without any encouragement to the persons being coached to elaborate, we can convey too strongly that we are in control of the conversation. The other person may become passive and simply wait to give another "yes" or "no" answer to the next closed probe.

Reflecting

Reflecting responses briefly restate what others have just said (content) or what others are feeling (emotions). Such responses communicate understanding and encourage the development of information. Some examples of statements and reflecting responses are found below:

> *Statement:* "I don't really understand what top management wants. They say our order of priorities is safety, quality, and schedule. But just let it look like a test is going to slip a day and all hell breaks loose."

> *Reflecting:* "It seems to you that you are getting mixed messages and it still looks to you as if schedule is number one."

Statement: "With all these changes hitting us at once, my group is in mass confusion. I'm sure tired of telling my people that I don't know any more than they do."

Reflecting: "From where you sit it feels like there are no answers to anything right now—just questions."

Statement: "All they do for supervisors is tell us what we can't do. We've got about as much power over our employees as I have over the Congress."

Reflecting: "You're expected to get the same amount of work out of your people, but with less and less clout."

In the hundreds of coaching training workshops that I have directed, I have observed over and over again that using reflecting responses is not a skill that comes naturally to people or that they learn easily. But reflecting is a skill of singular value in coaching. Some reasons for this are as follows:

1. To reflect we must listen. Reflecting forces listening and builds strong listening skills. We cannot restate or convey understanding of another's feelings unless we have first heard accurately what the other person has said.

2. Another value of reflecting responses is that they develop information even when they are not quite accurate or on target. When a reflecting response is off target, the person being coached will respond with a "no" and then clarify what he or she has said.

Indicating Respect

Indicating respect means that we behave in such a way that we stimulate the free and open development of information and do nothing to inhibit its flow. Using the kinds of behavior that are associated with good attending ensures that we indicate respect. Indicating respect also means that we avoid behaviors that communicate lack of respect. Here are a few examples of not indicating respect:

1. *Discounting.* These are behaviors that suggest to people that they are not individuals but that they belong to a larger class ("Everyone has the same sort of problem") or behaviors that communicate that a person is making too much of a problem ("It's not as big a deal as you are making it"). Both kinds of behaviors tend to depersonalize the other person. Examples of statements that discount follow:

   - "You are probably overreacting to what's happening."
   - "Your problem is one that all team leaders have to face."
   - "All new employees have trouble with that part of the procurement process."

2. *Ridiculing.* These are behaviors that exaggerate another person's mistakes or apparent failures. Examples of ridiculing behavior follow:

   - "Congratulations, Bob, I can only conclude from your behavior yesterday that you intended to find the most creative way possible to make the whole team look like fools to the vice president."
   - "I know you don't believe in dressing for success, but must you look like an unmade bed?"

3. *Being judgmental.* These are behaviors that communicate that you call the intentions of others into question or blame them for whatever may have happened. Some examples follow:

   - "If you thought the valve might fail, why didn't you replace it before you went home?"
   - "Maybe you just haven't tried hard enough to get along with the other guys."

- "I think you're misunderstanding what's going on. I can't believe our people have that kind of prejudice."

4. *Being irrelevant.* Irrelevant responses do not forward the progress of developing information because they tend to sidetrack the other person and encourage the person to provide information that is not *immediately* useful in clarifying the topic at hand. Irrelevant responses tend to reflect the coach's interest in his or her own agenda, rather than that of the other person. Some examples follow:

- "How long did you think about this problem before you decided to talk to me about it?"
- "I certainly don't feel the way you do about my job. I love coming to work."

One quality that we must consistently create in our coaching conversations is respect. We must learn to use behaviors that encourage a free exchange of opinions and information. We must learn to avoid behaviors that invite resistance or resentment and that block the exchange of information or ideas.

The following examples illustrate the differences between responses that indicate respect and those that do not. Note that the responses that indicate respect either stimulate the development of useful information or put no obstacle in the way of such development. In contrast, the responses that do not indicate respect do little to develop useful information or actually encourage the development of useless information.

CO-WORKER STATEMENT: I don't see how I can be expected to use one computer to do my work and a second one for the new network system.

NOT RESPECTFUL RESPONSE 1: Everyone seems to have that sort of problem with the new system. (discounting)

NOT RESPECTFUL RESPONSE 2: How is it that other people seem

to be able to make the system work and use two computers? (judgmental)

RESPECTFUL RESPONSE: What are the specific kinds of problems that you are having? (open probe)

CO-WORKER STATEMENT: I can't work with the new operator. It's easier to do the job alone than to try to teach him. I just don't have the time.

NOT RESPECTFUL RESPONSE 1: What's the operator's name? (irrelevant)

NOT RESPECTFUL RESPONSE 2: Nobody finds it easy. All of our people have the same problem. (discounting)

NOT RESPECTFUL RESPONSE 3: Yeah, I know just about where you put training operators in your list of priorities—somewhere after lunch and golf. (ridiculing)

RESPECTFUL RESPONSE: Let's review your work priorities and see exactly where the major conflicts exist. (open probe)

CO-WORKER STATEMENT: I thought I understood your priorities on safety training and that you really meant for all of my people to complete the new course before the end of the year. Now it looks like I made a mistake.

NOT RESPECTFUL RESPONSE 1: I thought you would make a sensible judgment to keep training from interfering with production. But I guess you couldn't figure that out. (judgmental)

NOT RESPECTFUL RESPONSE 2: What do you mean by mistake? (irrelevant)

RESPECTFUL RESPONSE: I can see how we could have failed to connect on this. Let's see how we can keep the critical numbers on the floor and still have the people trained in a reasonable period of time. (acknowledging, resourcing)

Self-Disclosure

Coaches might make self-disclosure statements to communicate that they have had an experience similar to the one that the other person is describing. Such statements, if they are brief and relevant, tend to encourage others to feel that they are talking to someone who can identify with their problem. The danger of using self-disclosure is that coaches may spend too much time describing their own experience, rather than staying focused on the other person's need to explore his or her experiences. Some sample self-disclosure responses follow:

- "I've felt like that."

- "A similar thing happened to me."

- "My first project ran into a similar problem."

Immediacy

During a coaching conversation, a number of things can occur that keep the conversation from progressing to a positive conclusion. The persons being coached may do any of the following:

- Display outbursts of strong emotions such as anger, hostility, fear, or anxiety

- Make little or no verbal response and not participate fully in the interaction

- Begin to cover the same ground over and over again

- Be surprised by some topic and need time to prepare to discuss it

- Become too tired or distracted to engage further in the conversation

Immediacy is the skill of being able to respond to "real time" conditions, such as those listed above. It is the skill of focusing the coaching conversation on the here and now. It includes any comment that draws *immediate* attention to anything that could block the progress of the coaching session.

. . . .

I once observed a manager conducting a coaching session with a co-worker. The manager was trying to encourage the co-worker to provide more technical direction on a project that he was leading. The two kept going around and around without reaching a solution. The manager's perspective was that the co-worker knew more about the project's technical requirements than anyone else. The co-worker's position was that his job was to manage several projects and that he could not become too involved in the technology of any one project. Finally, the manager employed the skill of immediacy and said, "Look, we're not getting anywhere. All we are doing is restating our positions. This project is in technical trouble. I need your help. How about thinking about the problem—what you want and what I need—and then getting together again tomorrow to see if we can't find a solution."

. . . .

Immediacy means not only drawing attention to blocks that develop during coaching interactions, but it also means offering strategies for overcoming these blocks. Such strategies may include

- Deferring the conversation to a later time

- Pausing for a moment to give people a chance to collect their thoughts

- Approaching the problem from a different angle

- Acknowledging that the coach and persons being coached should try to find a compromise

The following are a few examples of what the skill of immediacy sounds like:

- "I think we've started going over the same ground again. Maybe we've pretty much exhausted the reasons for the slip in schedule and need to start looking for remedies."

- "I have the sense that I'm not doing much to help you find the kind of information you want. Is that the case, or am I just being overly sensitive?"

- "I had hoped we could talk about the problems we are having with the new spreadsheet, but what's most on your mind is your disappointment about not receiving the kind of bonus you expected. How can we get at your problem as well as mine?"

Summarizing

Sound coaching behavior includes stopping the flow of the conversation and summarizing what has been said. Summarizing helps both coaches and those being coached to keep the key facts before them and to ensure mutual understanding.

Examples of what summarizing sounds like follow:

- "You have had a sudden increase in your workload; you're losing your best lead engineer; and there is confusion about priorities. These seem to be the major reasons we've fallen behind schedule on the new software package. Is that about it?"

- "Let me see if I've got this. You feel that the two of us have stopped working closely together on the survey design, you have the sense that I'm avoiding you or don't want to work with you, and it's hard for you to know how to contribute. Are those the issues here?"

Process Stage I: Involving

_{p44}

You will notice in Exhibit 3.1 that the process model is separated into three stages: involving, developing, and resolving. Each stage has two subheadings: goals and skills specific to the stage. In the final column to the right the general skills are listed, indicating that they have general use throughout the coaching process. These skills were described in some depth above. In this section the goals for each stage and the stage-specific skills that are particularly relevant to achieving the goals of the stage are described.

The stages in the process mark the transition from one set of goals to the next. It is a coach's awareness that the goals of one stage have been met that signal that it is time to move the process forward to the next stage.

Stage I Goals

Involving describes the initial stage of a coaching conversation in Process 1. The goals that the coach should have in mind at this stage are these:

- To clarify the purpose of the conversation—what is being discussed, the expected outcomes, and the like

- To involve the person being coached in a free and easy interaction

- To clarify any important ground rules or constraints, such as time, confidentiality, roles and responsibilities, and the like

- To develop comfort and trust

Specific Skills for Stage I

Only one specific skill for Stage 1 requires mention—clarifying. Coaches have the responsibility to establish as quickly as possible the purpose of the conversation. If the other person has initiated the session, then clarification begins to take place after the other person has made some attempt to say what he or she needs. If the coach has initiated the conversation, then clarification begins with the coach making some statement about the purpose of the conversation. Clarification may sound like the following:

- "I gather you must be having some problems with the new quality assurance procedures. Tell me what the difficulty is."

- "I would like to help you figure out what one or two jobs would be the best for you to seek next."

- "There are three key steps in the new procedure. I would like to make sure that you are satisfied and that you understand them before we finish our conversation."

- "I have the feeling that you aren't comfortable yet giving orders to the people who once were your peers. If I'm right I'd like to help in any way I can."

Process Stage II: Developing

Stage II Goals

All the stages in Coaching Process 1: Responding to Needs vary in the kinds of topics covered and information developed. If it is a *counseling* conversation, the emphasis in Stage II will be to develop information that leads to a common understanding of and the probable causes of a problem. If it is a *mentoring* conversation, the purpose of Stage II will be to help the person being coached understand such things as a company's culture or strategies for developing a career. If the coaching conversation focuses on *instruction*, then the focus of Stage II will be on teaching new knowledge or skills. Whatever topic or content is being developed, one or more of these goals is characteristic of Stage II: developing information; gaining insight; defining the problem and causes; or achieving new learning.

Specific Skills for Stage II

All of the general skills help develop information, insight, and learning—the goals of Stage II. In addition to the general skills relevant throughout the process, two stage-specific skills contribute to successful movement through Stage II: resourcing and confirming.

Resourcing

Coaches are sources of help. Being sources of help, however, does not always mean that we know more about some subject than the persons we are trying to help. Being a successful coach always means that we are masters of the processes of helping and that we have the skills to create and maintain a successful coaching interaction. The help that occurs through coaching, as often as not, occurs through the process of helping others discover what they already know. There will, however, be many times when coaches can and should serve as resources. Resources will take such forms as giving information, advice, instruction, a demonstration, or a referral. Two characteristics of resourcing require some elaboration:

Dependency. Resourcing should never preempt the other person's initiative or create dependence on the coach. The strength of coaching lies in the fact that coaches are potential resources. But this very fact can also be a weakness. The best people in every organization are problem solvers. They have been rewarded and promoted because they have demonstrated their ability to solve problems. The more qualified a person is in solving problems, the more that person will take the lead in solving the problems of others—even when they should not do so.

Concrete. As I have already shown, one of the characteristics of successful coaches is that they speak in concrete terms and they encourage others to think and speak in concrete terms. Being concrete is particularly relevant to resourcing. Coaches are not being resources when they tell others to "try harder," "clean up the report," "find yourself a good model," or "you need to network." Such comments are too vague to be of much use. Concrete resourcing sounds like the following: "John knows more about this subject than anyone; how about asking him for some help," "Projects are getting so important around here that I strongly suggest that you consider signing up for the next course we bring in-house."

It is never to the advantage of an organization to have people overly dependent on the knowledge, skills, or experience of others. Interdependency, on the other hand, is highly desirable and is a characteristic of high-performing teams. Dependency can create people who are too fearful to make their own decisions and test their own ideas. Every time we have a coaching conversation with a co-worker we face a choice. Will we give the other person every opportunity to solve the problem, or will we solve the problem for him or her? Will we give the other person the opportunity to discover new knowledge, or will we help the other person become more and more dependent on us for knowledge. Every time we resolve some unknown for another person, we may be missing an opportunity to develop the competence and confidence of that person. Coaching is always an opportunity to empower others by helping them to solve their own problems, take responsibility for their own learning, and find new opportunities to exert competent influence. Resourcing must never be used to subvert the need for others to take responsibility for their own performance and success.

Confirming

A second stage-specific skill is confirming, employed by coaches to make sure that information has been received and understood, that insight and learning have occurred, and that follow-on plans are clear. Confirming often takes the form of asking for feedback and includes the many ways that a coach may ask others to repeat what common understanding or agreement has been developed. Here are a few examples of what confirming may sound like:

- "How about going over these steps in your own words and telling me how you will proceed."

- "Based on what we have covered, what do you see now as the key points that should be covered in your next status review?"

- "I would like to test what I think each of us has agreed to do before we meet with our project leader tomorrow."

When some new knowledge or skill is being learned in a coaching conversation, coaches may confirm that learning has occurred by asking the other person to demonstrate what has been learned. Following are some examples of this kind of confirming:

- "Based on what we've been talking about, how about making a few entries in the database on your own?"

- "Now that we've covered some of the mistakes that people typically make in writing a technical report, let's look at this one and see how many mistakes jump out at you."

- "How about doing a practice run-through for me of your presentation tomorrow, including all the changes that we have agreed on."

Process Stage III: Resolving

Stage III Goals

The goals in Stage III depend, of course, on the content and purpose of the coaching conversation. These goals could include problem resolution, next steps, commitment, positive relationship, and closure. The general and overarching goals of coaching are always to obtain people's commitment to sustained superior performance—while maintaining positive work relationships between the coach and the persons being coached. The entire process leads toward these goals, and they are included in Stage III to emphasize again that they are the two primary goals of all coaching interactions.

Commitment is built throughout the conversation as coaches do such things as develop clarity, build competency, extend influence, and express appreciation. *Positive relationships* are developed, maintained, and strengthened throughout a conversation by coaches having the discipline to use the process and create the fundamental characteristics of successful coaching, such as communicating respect, ensuring that the conversation is mutual, focusing on the problem, and staying future oriented.

Besides building commitment and maintaining positive relationships, *problem resolution, next steps,* and *closure* are also goals of Stage III. *Problem resolution* means identifying what steps or resources are required to solve the problems discussed. Planning *next steps* can take a number of different forms, depending on the content of the coaching conversation. If it is a *counseling* conversation, the other person and coach will identify strategies for the other person's use to resolve the problems identified in Stage II. If it is a *mentoring* conversation, the next steps may be for the other person to test what have been identified as important characteristics of the organization's culture and for the coach and other person to meet again and discuss what has been verified and what has not been verified about the culture. In the case of *tutoring,* the next steps may be for the other person to practice the new learning or to work at some additional learning projects on his or her own.

Closure describes the process of completing the coaching conversation. The goal is to reinforce the other person's sense of achievement. Closure is effected by reviewing what has transpired during the coaching conversation and by affirming the other person's strengths.

Specific Skills for Stage III

In addition to the general skills of the process, three other skills have special utility for rounding out the whole interaction and for reinforcing the achievement of the general goals of commitment and positive relationships, as well as the specific goals of planning next steps and closure. These skills are *reviewing, planning,* and *affirming.*

Reviewing

Developing information, resolving a problem, and gaining new learning are results that the other person will typically achieve from successful coaching conversations. What has been accomplished or what agreements have been made should be reviewed at the end of the coaching conversation. Reviewing ensures common understanding and reinforces what the other person has achieved. Reviewing builds a sense of completeness and closure. It also encourages a visible display of the other person's commitment. Reviewing may take such forms as the following:

- "I think you've done a good job identifying the main reasons that we are behind in getting the new proposal out. See if this is correct. We didn't receive clarification on the request for a proposal until two weeks after we requested it. The new cost estimate software turned out to have some pretty severe bugs. And your team hasn't had a chance to gel because of so many personnel changes."

- "I think we have our strategy pretty well together for our meeting with the Personnel Advisory Committee. First, we won't take the lead in attacking the new time card policy. This is the general manager's own idea, so we want to go softly. Second, if the policy is brought

up, we will comment first on its positive features.
Third, when we do start talking about changes, we will
make sure that we show how the changes we want are
primarily ways of cutting down paperwork."

- "I want to make sure that we are together about how
  our team should behave in these technical reviews with
  the suppliers: First, we should give a brief statement of
  what we have found that needs to be changed and the
  data to support the need. Second, we should always
  make a recommendation of how to fix what we think is
  wrong."

Planning

In the final stage of a coaching conversation, coaches plan with the
people being coached such things as the following:

- Strategies to resolve the problems identified

- Methods to test or build on the other person's understanding of the company's culture

- Ways to test new learning or opportunities for additional learning

- Actions to improve performance or take on new
  responsibility

Planning can be as simple as having the person being coached
try out some new learning and then check back with the coach. Or
it can be as complicated as having the other person prepare a five-
or ten-year career development sequence. It can include tasks such
as putting together a revised project schedule or writing a proposal.
Whatever the content or complexity of a plan, good plans tend to
have the following characteristics:

- They are developed with full involvement of the person being coached. They ensure that the other person assumes responsibility for the plan and that it reflects that person's input and decisions.

- They are concrete and do more than convey vague intentions to "try harder," "be more sensitive," or "pay more attention to senior managers."

- They have built-in means of measuring their progress and success in the future.

The following are some of the kinds of things that can be said to ensure successful planning:

- "I suggest that you try your new approach with John, giving him more latitude in the sequence that he uses in handling applications. See how it goes for a week, and then get back with me and let's see how it's going."

- "After you've had a chance to find out from our rate clerks exactly what they do, what they like, and what they don't like, let's talk again and see if you want to make that move. But plan to see me no later than ten days from now."

- "I'm delighted that you wanted to learn more about my job in this budgeting sequence. How about getting together next Monday and continuing our conversation?"

Affirming

One general goal of all successful coaching is to achieve commitment to sustained superior performance. Commitment results from four conditions: clarity, competency, influence, and appreciation. Affirming is a skill for reinforcing the sense of competency in the persons being coached and for expressing appreciation for their performance.

Affirming draws special attention to what the other person has done during the coaching interaction. In a successful coaching conversation, the person being coached will typically demonstrate a variety of current and newly acquired strengths. The skill of affirming draws explicit attention to these strengths. Affirming might sound like the following:

- "I know it wasn't easy for us to dig into the causes for the team's poor performance this quarter. But everyone has done a fine job of analysis. I think our team has shown a lot of courage in what we've done. I, for one, feel that we can see the light at the end of the tunnel."

- "You're really developing a feel for what makes this division work. Researchers are a funny lot, and you're clearly getting a handle on what makes us tick."

- "I think that you're well over the toughest part of this new procurement sequence. You've gone through it faster than I did."

Summary of Coaching Process 1: Responding to Needs

The stages of Process 1, the general skills that support the whole process, the goals, and the skills specific to each stage of the process have been covered. The key points to remember about the process and skills are as follows:

1. Coaching Process 1 describes what typically goes on in successful coaching conversations when the emphasis is on counseling, mentoring, or tutoring.

2. Coaching Process 1 has three stages:

- Stage I: Involving
- Stage II: Developing
- Stage III: Resolving

3. The general flow of the process is the same, regardless of the emphasis or content.

4. All stages of the process are interdependent, and there is typically movement back and forth between the stages. However, the process is directional; it does move toward specific results and closure.

5. A set of general skills supports the whole process, and certain stage-specific skills are needed in the various stages.

6. It is the *process* of the coaching conversation and not the content that leads to a commitment to higher performance while maintaining positive work relationships between coach and co-worker.

As I have presented the goals, stages, and skills of Process 1, I have provided a number of illustrations in order to leave you, the reader, with as concrete a picture as possible of the coaching conversation. But it is the total coaching conversation that produces the desired results most consistently. To be competent coaches, we must be able to carry the process through from beginning to end. It is important, therefore, to illustrate Process 1 in its entirety.

Examples of Coaching Process 1: Responding to Needs

The next three sections of this chapter provide examples of Process 1 when the emphasis is on counseling, mentoring, or tutoring. In the examples, "C" is the symbol used for coach. "O" stands for the other person, the one being coached. The person doing the coaching can be anyone who wants to take on this function and is permitted to do so.

The left-hand column records a coaching conversation. In the right-hand column, the stages and skills of the process are identified. Not all the skills are illustrated in each example, just as not all skills would always be used in any specific coaching conversation.

How to Use the Examples

The examples illustrate the goals, stages, and skills for the three coaching functions of counseling, mentoring, and tutoring. These examples can be powerful learning tools and help with the transfer of learning to on-the-job application of effective and efficient coaching practices. Use the following approach for the best results.

1. Before you read through an example, review Process 1—the stages, goals, general skills, and specific skills listed in Exhibit 3.1.

2. Cover up the right-hand column of the examples and test your ability to identify the stages and skills.

3. After you have gone through an example once, read through the example again and substitute your own alternative responses for the ones the coach makes in the example.

Counseling Example

Counseling is a problem-solving conversation that many be initiated by a manager or subordinate. Typical of the specific outcomes that counseling may achieve are the following:

- Accurate descriptions of problems and their causes

- Technical and organizational insight

- Venting of strong feelings

- Changes in points of view

- Commitment to self-sufficiency

- Deeper personal insight about one's feelings and behavior

Commitment and positive work relationships are always outcomes of all successful coaching sessions—regardless of the specific coaching function involved.

Counseling Conversation	*Comments*
O: John, when you have trouble getting your suppliers to deliver what they say they will, what do you do?	*Stage I: Involving*
C: What kind of problems are you having?	*Stage II: Developing* Open probe
O: The main problem is that every time MasterCom upgrades the hardware on our desktops or installs a new piece of software, we end up finding problems, we end up with our work stations down, and waste time having MasterCom redo the work.	
C: So it's a recurring problem that what work MasterCom does is not reliable.	Reflecting
O: Right. But every time I complain, what I hear are a lot of excuses like we put them on too short a turnaround time, or we didn't specify clearly enough what we wanted, or the problem is not with them, but with the manufacturers.	

C: The contractor doesn't accept responsibility for the screw-ups.

Reflecting

O: It's not quite that clean. Sometimes we're told that they're having a problem with inexperienced people. And I guess we did expand our contract with them so that they had to hire a lot of new people in hurry.

C: MasterCom is doing too much work that has to be redone. They're creating downtime for you, along with a good bit of aggravation. I guess it makes you uncertain about what's going to happen when you give them a job to do.

Summarizing

O: Right. I can't fire them. The contract is for everyone who needs computer support, not just our group. I have to use them, no matter what.

C: Do you have any idea about how other groups are being served? Are other people complaining?

Closed probes

O: That's the funny part. Everyone else who uses them seems to be pretty happy.

C: Is it safe to assume that this is a problem that is special to your group?

Closed probe

O: It would appear so. At least the problem is bad enough for me to want to fix it.

C: What are some reasons that you can think of for the problem being confined to your group? — Open probe

O: Well, I can think of one or two. Maybe our jobs are getting worked on by some of MasterCom's newest people. Or maybe there is some missing step in their own quality assurance process. Maybe our jobs aren't checked properly. Or maybe they keep us at the bottom of their job list and wait until the last minute to work on our stuff. I guess there must be some other possibilities, but I can't come up with any right now.

C: I gather from what you're saying that we don't know for sure what's causing the problem. — Reflecting

O: I guess that's right.

C: So the first step is to make sure you understand the problem. Got any ideas of how to go about finding out? — *Stage III: Resolving* / Acknowledging / Open probe

O: I've already had some meetings with their manager who has the responsibility, but it's clear that hasn't helped much.

C: Maybe you need to get everybody involved who works on your jobs with your own people who give them the work. — Resourcing

O: Well it's worth a try. I'm sure they have a different picture than we do about what's going on.

C: Got any idea when you might have a meeting organized?	Next steps Open probe

O: I think I'll start on it when I get back to my office. We sure can't live with what's going on now.

C: One thing about bringing everybody together who is involved is that you'll have the people together who know how to fix the problem. I guess you've decided now that you know what the problem looks like, but you don't know for sure what the causes are. A meeting is a good place to start. I'll be interested to know what happens. Give me a call next week.	Resourcing Reviewing Affirming Planning

O: I'll do that, and thanks.

Mentoring Example

Mentoring is a coaching conversation that may be initiated by a person needing help or a person who offers help. It uses Coaching Process 1: Responding to Needs and differs from counseling and tutoring only in content. It results in information that permits people to become more fully integrated into a company's culture and to further their own success. Mentoring is sage advice that unlocks organizational mysteries. It is a process of helping people share in those insights that managers have gained from personal experience. Mentoring permits people to avoid pitfalls, to plan their careers, and to adjust their behaviors to fit cultural norms. Typical outcomes of mentoring are as follows:

- Development of political savvy

- Sensitivity to an organization's culture

- Personal networking

- Sensitivity to senior managers' likes and dislikes

- Commitment to organizational goals and values

- Commitment to managing one's own development and career

Mentoring Conversation	*Comments*
C: Martha, I think it's time for you to consider expanding your experience and learning more about the whole company. It's pretty easy right now to move around and take some temporary positions. Here's a notice I received yesterday calling for volunteers to spend six months in personnel.	*Stage I: Involving* Clarifying Resourcing
O: I don't mind the thought of learning about what other departments are doing, but I'm an engineer. I'm not too keen on the idea of spending time in personnel. There's so much happening now in new materials, smart systems, sensors, and other areas that really interest me.	*Stage II: Developing*
C: Your big concern is moving too far away from engineering, but I seem to	Reflecting

hear you say that working in personnel may not be all that useful.

O: Well, I would be less than truthful if I didn't say that I think being an engineer is a cut above working in personnel.

C: I guess it's where you see yourself in five to ten years that matters. Do you want to spend your career as a hands-on engineer or do you expect to aspire to being the person who manages a few hundred hands-on engineers?

Resourcing
Closed probes

O: Well, I like being an engineer right now, but I certainly have aspirations. I want to go as far as my talents and hard work will take me. Yeah, I hope to be a manager someday.

C: Have you thought much about what managers at my level do?

Closed probe

O: I can't say that I've given it a lot of thought. I know from trying to contact you at times that you must spend most of your life in meetings.

C: No question about the meetings. But I spend most of my time finding the right people, rewarding them, and handling people problems. The two toughest jobs are finding the right people and taking care of them and finding them the resources they need to do their work. People and money— that's what everything comes down to.

Self-disclosure
Resourcing

O: When you put it like that, I guess
I would do well to learn how personnel does its business. But there's no
chance I would be stuck there is
there?

C: Not a chance. You, I, and the   Resourcing
director of personnel would sign a
contract. You would be on loan for
six months and then come back to
your group. You are assured of coming
back to your old job or one of equal
interest to you.

O: I'd like to think about this a bit   *Stage III: Resolving*
more. It sounds like something I
should do. Who else has done this
sort of thing? Maybe I could talk to
him or her.

C: I think those are both good ideas.   Affirming
Dean Hensley from the test lab did a   Resourcing
stint with procurement last year. You
could discuss this with him.

O: Okay, I'll do that.

C: I think you understand what I   Affirming
consider to be a real opportunity for
you. I believe you have some sense of
just how important learning how
personnel works is. I know from
working with you the past few years
that you will give what we have talked
about very thoughtful consideration.
How about meeting with me   Planning
next Friday to let me know what
you've decided. In the meantime, if

you want to talk some more with me, I'll be happy to do that.

O: Thanks for your interest. I'll get back to you on Friday, or earlier if I have any questions.

Tutoring Example

Tutoring is the personal process of teaching individuals or small groups such as teams. Tutoring also uses Process 1: Responding to Needs. It differs only in content. This coaching conversation may be initiated by people who recognize their learning needs or by people who recognize the learning needs of others and want to help meet these needs. It should always be concerned with conveying learning that has immediate impact on the way a job is currently performed. It is a waste of time to tutor people in knowledge and skills that they may apply *someday*. Even though tutoring has a strong orientation to the present, it shares with all coaching functions the goal of long-term commitment. The final goal of tutoring is the long-term commitment of people to their own learning. Typical examples of outcomes from tutoring conversations are as follows:

- Increased technical competence

- Increased breadth of technical understanding

- Movement to an expert status

- Increased learning pace

- Commitment to continuous learning

Tutoring Conversation	Comments
C: You've just had your first crack at using the new company requirements for planning a project. How did it go?	*Stage I: Involving* Clarifying Open probe

O: I am not out of the woods, but I think I've made a good start.

C: Anything I could help you with?   *Stage II: Developing*
Open probe

O: I think the things that are the most bothersome are not so much the technical definitions and work procedures, but I could really use some help in getting the team to start working as a team.

C: It's easy to see why forming the   Acknowledging
team could raise some questions. About the only help you get from the requirements is that you're supposed to develop the team. What specific things do you want to know   Open probe
more about?

O: Right now I need to know how to help the people to think of themselves as a team and to be responsive to each other—being more concerned about the whole project, rather than with each person's job assignment.

C: Sounds as though everyone   Reflecting
doesn't have the same idea of what being a team means.

O: I think you're right.

C: Here's a set of steps that I have   *Stage III: Resolving*
followed in developing my own teams.   Resourcing
You might want to test these with your project team. You'll notice that the

first thing listed is for the team to agree on a set of working norms.

O: I suppose norms are the ground rules that govern how we expect each person to function as a team member. What norms have you found useful?

C: What has been useful for me may not be what your team needs. The norms must be theirs. Norms are no good unless they have been built by consensus. But, from what you've said, you will probably want to have a norm about responsiveness—one that states just how each person will react to requests for help from other team members.

Self-disclosure

Resourcing

O: I like the idea of saying up front just how we will work together. Could be that we just haven't made that explicit enough and I counted on what I thought was obvious.

C: I think you've isolated what you need to know to get started with your team, which is to set team norms. You already have the most important thing, which is your own desire to develop the team. When do you think you'll have a chance to help the team to set some norms?

Affirming

Planning

O: We always have a team on Friday afternoon. That should be a good time to start.

C: Good luck. Give me a call after   Planning
your meeting and let me know how
things turned out.

Key Learning Points for Chapter Three

1. Successful coaching conversations share a number of common
   characteristics:

   - The conversation satisfies the logical and psychological
     needs of the people involved.
   - The process is interactive and depends on the skills of the
     coach.
   - Coaching processes have interdependent stages; the goals
     of one stage must be met before the goals of the following
     stages can be met.

2. The three stages of Coaching Process 1: Responding to Needs
   and their goals are as follows:

   - Stage I: Involving: clear expectations, comfort, and trust
   - Stage II: Developing: information, insight, and learning
   - Stage III: Resolving: closure, next steps, positive relation-
     ship, and commitment

3. A set of general skills supports the whole process, and certain
   skills are specific to the various stages.

4. The process of the coaching conversation and not the content leads to a commitment to higher performance—while
   maintaining positive work relationships between coach and
   co-worker.

4

. . . .

Coaching Process 2:
Initiating Alternatives

Two generic processes support most extended coaching interactions. The first of these, Responding to Needs (described in the previous chapter), supports the coaching conversations concerned with counseling, mentoring, and tutoring. The second coaching process, Initiating Alternatives, supports the many kinds of confrontations that coaches make to raise the performance of their co-workers to higher levels or to correct a performance deficiency.

Confronting includes a wide range of interactions. At one end of the range are those in which a coach wants to encourage a co-worker who is performing successfully to accept more demanding tasks or greater responsibilities. At the other end of the range are those coaching interactions in which a coach addresses problems with a co-worker's performance.

All coaching conversations share the long-term goals of building people's commitment to sustained superior performance and of maintaining positive relationships between the coach and persons coached. Some examples of confronting people to move them to higher levels of performance are encouraging a systems manager to take on the more responsible position of project manager, or helping a mechanic to become a team leader, or challenging a data collection clerk to take on the job of analyst. Confrontations about less than satisfactory performance have goals such as helping co-workers to follow standard work rules, encouraging them to adhere to the work norms of a team, correcting their errors in computation, or asking them to adhere to quality standards.

Coaching conversations aimed at improving unsatisfactory performance are, of course, more difficult than ones that challenge people to take on more demanding work. The latter will usually be viewed positively by co-workers. However, telling co-workers that they are not performing a task at a satisfactory level will rarely be received positively. In cases in which a superior makes such a confrontation, the other person will often perceive the conversation (at least initially) as a reprimand.

Most of the material in this chapter will focus on the more difficult of the two kinds of confrontation. If coaches master the more difficult aspects of confrontation, they will certainly master the less difficult task of challenging co-workers to ever higher levels of achievement.

Before we look at Coaching Process 2: Initiating Alternatives, it may be useful to distinguish confrontation from criticism and to describe the ways in which we often make confrontation more difficult than it needs to be.

Confrontation and Criticism

Confrontation is a coaching process by which coaches create positive changes in performance and develop commitment to continuous improvement. As with all successful coaching, they do this while maintaining their positive relationships with the persons being coached. Initiating alternatives as a coaching activity means facing problems squarely and humanely, rather than facing them defiantly or antagonistically. It is a skilled and disciplined process for managing performance.

Confrontation can be confused with criticism. Criticism is not a coaching activity. It is counterproductive, and it does not have a high probability of leading to improved performance and commitment to higher levels of performance. Coaches must be especially sensitive to the differences between the two (see Figure 4.1).

Problem Versus Person

Confrontation focuses on a specific performance problem. It identifies concretely an improvement that the coach believes must be made. It addresses a performance issue that can be described and understood by both coach and co-worker. Criticism, on the other hand, focuses on the personal characteristics of a person—his or her attitudes and personal traits. Criticism faults the person for some weakness. The examples below contrast focus on the problem (confrontation) with focus on the person (criticism):

> *Problem:* "I've marked in your report a few grammatical mistakes. They are largely problems in nonagreement. I would appreciate your fixing them and giving me a corrected copy of the report by this afternoon."

> *Person:* "Your report demonstrates again just how little attention you give to detail."

> *Problem:* "I expected your budget estimate yesterday. When do you think it will be ready?"

> *Person:* "It looks like you don't care how much you inconvenience the rest of us by being late with your budget estimate."

Figure 4.1. Confrontation Versus Criticism

Problem: "Your telling the vice president at our status meeting this morning that she didn't have her facts right clearly ticked her off and didn't help our cause much. I'd like to figure out a strategy with you that protects your integrity, but doesn't encourage hostility from senior management."

Person: "You demonstrated zero sensitivity to our relationship with the vice president. You seem to be determined to put us in the worst possible light every time you get the chance."

Specific Versus General

Confrontation identifies precisely what the coach thinks should be different. Even when the problem may be a recurring one, confrontation starts with the most recent specific example of the undesired performance. The coach says, "I see X, but what we need is Y." Criticism tends to be general. It often takes a single error or mistake and magnifies it into a widespread or typical behavior. Criticism includes words like always, never, typically, or continuously. The examples that follow contrast being specific (confrontation) with being general (criticism):

Specific: "Your time card shows that you have been late four out of the last six work days. I need everyone here at eight. Being here on time is part of your job."

General: "You just persist in not doing anything right. No matter how many times I tell you, you fail to submit your time card."

Specific: "I haven't received your revised timetable for the move. I need it no later than tomorrow so that I can coordinate the whole department's move."

General: "As far as I can see you've done nothing to help us make this move."

Specific: "I think you know that we all need to stay late on the days we receive our system performance updates. We have to make the modifications and have the system up and running by the next morning shift. The team needed you yesterday, but you left early."

General: "You never try to go the extra mile. Everyone else knows we all must stay late to bring our system on line by morning, but I never see you around after four o'clock."

Change Versus Blame

Confrontation is focused on improvement. Coaches who know how to confront are clearly focused on the performance change that they want. They are not interested in apologies or guilt. They do not want co-workers to feel weak and pessimistic. They want their co-workers to decide to improve and to believe that they can do so. Confrontation always is focused on what can be changed—the future.

Criticism, on the other hand, is used to establish blame. When we criticize we ask others to feel guilty for what they have done or left undone. Notice in the comparisons below the difference between a focus on blame and on change:

Blame: "The lack of sensitivity that you demonstrated in being late for our review meeting this morning has caused our team a lot of embarrassment. How could you do such a thing?"

Change: "You were late for our review meeting this morning. I can't complete the process without you. I would like to know how we can keep this from happening again."

Blame: "Why did you leave the printers running last night? What have you got to do that's so important that you can't take time to shut them down before you leave?"

Change: "I noticed the printers were still on when I came in this morning. According to the security log, you were the last one to leave. I'd like to figure out a way to make sure that our printers are turned off each evening."

Relationship Versus Self

A general criterion for all successful coaching is that, while achieving change and commitment, it also maintains or improves positive work relationships between a coach and the persons being coached. In the case of confrontations about performance problems, maintaining positive relationships can become quite difficult. Confrontation's focus on relationships puts it in sharp contrast to criticism. Criticism focuses on the needs of the person doing the criticizing.

When we criticize, we are driven by our own needs "to let go," "to speak our minds," or "to tell someone off." We are often angry when we criticize and are responding largely to our own need to vent this anger.

Remember that confrontation is a tool for improving performance and that criticism is not. One way to think about improving our confrontation skills is to remind ourselves just how much confrontation differs from criticism.

Added Difficulties

Confronting performance problems in a way that results in positive change and commitment while maintaining positive relationships is not easy. We do, however, often make confronting a lot more difficult than it need be. Some of the difficulties that we add to the coaching process of confronting follow:

1. We avoid confronting problems almost completely, and, when we do confront, we use confrontation as a strategy of last resort.

2. We fail to establish clear performance expectations with our co-workers that would eliminate as much vagueness and uncertainty as possible.

3. We fail to give timely and sufficient feedback that permits co-workers to know how we perceive their performance.

4. We fail to express sufficient uncontaminated appreciation for the achievements of our co-workers.

Avoidance

In the coaching workshops that I conduct, I often ask participants to tell me what words or phrases they associate with "confrontation." Their responses always suggest various negative associations. They link with confrontation such thoughts as "being angry," "creating bad feelings," "feeling resentment," "fighting," "becoming disturbed," and so on. It is apparent that confronting performance problems is often a painful experience for many of us and something that we would like to avoid.

One example of avoidance that I will always remember involved a bank president who contacted me about conducting training in interpersonal relations and communications for his senior staff and loan executives. When I met the president he confided the following:

> I plan to retire in two years. The board and I have decided that Gerald will take my place. He's extremely competent. He's probably the best loan coach that the bank has ever had. He knows the bank's whole operation from top to bottom. There is just one thing. A lot of our clients are farmers. Sometimes he seems to offend them. We receive complaints from time to time. It's possible that he could lose out and we would have to select someone else to take my place. He's just insensitive to people sometimes. I've contacted you because I would like to see

if we might help Gerald. I just don't have the heart to
tell him what I hear. I know how hurt he would be if I
ever said anything to him. I don't want to single him out
as the one person who needs the training—so I thought
you might do something for all my senior people.

Few of us will ever resort to so involved a stratagem to avoid confrontation, but too many of us do avoid timely confrontation. We
avoid it because we associate so many of our own negative emotions
with it and have a fear of causing negative feelings in our co-workers.

When we are confronted, we will typically feel that we are under
verbal attack. The most typical responses to verbal attack are (1)
to become passive and withdraw; (2) to make excuses and ratio-
nalize; or (3) to take the offensive and strike back. All three represent some sort of defense or resistance. This potential for resistance
makes many of us uncomfortable at the idea of confrontation. The
more emotion that is displayed in the resistance of the persons being
confronted, the more uncomfortable we become.

Fear often leads us to avoid confronting performance problems.
Avoiding confrontation because we are afraid of a negative reaction
ultimately makes the process even more difficult. Avoidance results
in delay, and delay usually ensures that performance problems will
become more complex and less manageable.

It is apparent that if we could learn to confront in a way that
both limits negative reactions and manages them when they do
occur, we would not so often put off confronting poor performance.
One of the key characteristics of Coaching Process 2: Initiating
Alternatives is that it provides a way for limiting and managing negative reactions.

Performance Expectations

Another way that we make it difficult to confront performance
problems is that we do not make sure that we have a clear understanding with our co-workers of what we expect of one another. Per-

formance can only be honestly and successfully managed when performance expectations are clear. Without such standards, confrontation can become both senseless and arbitrary.

I once was asked to observe a general manager for personnel conduct a coaching conversation with a supervisor who reported to him and to give feedback to the general manager. What follows is the first part of the conversation that I recorded. G represents the general manager and S the supervisor.

> G: I'm still not convinced that you are taking hold of your group the way I want you to.
>
> S: I've really tried to take hold and do what you expect. I really believe I'm making progress.
>
> G: I know that you are trying. I just don't feel that you are managing. I want people in your position to be more professional—to show that they are real professional leaders.
>
> S: Do you mean I'm too friendly with my people? It's really hard to be too distant from people who have been in the company as long as I have.
>
> G: No, I'm not asking you to quit being friendly. But you've got to get your people to look up to you as their leader. They need to see you as the person who is in charge.
>
> S: Well, I certainly want to be respected. I want to be more professional. I'll just have to keep giving it my very best. Anything in particular that you want me to do?
>
> G: I think that you must change the general impression that you make and be more forceful when you hold your staff meetings and things like that.

The conversation never became more concrete or helpful. The general manager began the coaching conversation without ever having established any clear performance expectations, and he ended the conversation the same way that he had begun it. It was as though the general manager were telling the supervisor, "Go get me a rock." How could the struggling supervisor ever expect to find the right rock?

At the end of the coaching conversation, the supervisor had no clearer idea of what was expected than he did before the conversation started. What is even more detrimental is that the general manager truly imagined that he had confronted the supervisor about his performance. He fully believed that the supervisor now knew what he was not doing and what he should start doing.

I have often observed members of work teams confront one another about poor cooperation, poor communication, or some other performance problem. At the same time I have observed how confused these confrontations become and how little good they do because these teams have never set down exactly what members can expect from one another and exactly how they will work together.

Successful confrontation is, at best, a difficult task. But the lack of clear performance expectations adds another order of magnitude to the difficulty of the task.

Feedback

As discussed, two ways that we add unnecessary difficulties when confronting are by (1) avoiding confronting in a timely way, thereby letting small problems become much bigger ones, and (2) not clarifying performance expectations with co-workers. A third way that we create difficulties is by failing to establish feedback as an expected norm so that members in our work groups will know exactly how their work is perceived by their colleagues.

Feedback is the routine process by which we continuously "close the loop" between expectations and performance. It is a process of both requesting information and giving information. By requesting information, we obtain the perceptions of co-workers about our own performance. By giving information we give co-workers our perceptions of how well they are doing. One of the strongest team development tools available is 360-degree feedback in the team, by which every member receives regular feedback from every other member.

The key characteristics of effective feedback are that it is *timely* and *sufficient*. We know that feedback has not been sufficient when we hear such concerns expressed as: "I wish I had known," "Why didn't you tell me?," "When did we start falling behind?," and "That comes as a big surprise to me." We know that feedback has not been timely when we hear expressions like: "But I thought you told me earlier that . . .," "What you are telling me today is sure different from what you said yesterday," and "When did we change the milestones?"

I have never met anyone in any organization who intended to fail. I doubt that any of us ever go to work saying to ourselves, "Hot dog, another chance to embarrass myself." Feedback gives all of us the opportunity to do what we want to do—take an active role in managing our own performance and ensuring that our performance meets the expectations of our co-workers.

Feedback gives people the opportunity to adjust their performance. When feedback is timely and sufficient, confrontation may never be required. When feedback is not timely and not sufficient, confrontation becomes unnecessarily more difficult.

Uncontaminated Appreciation

A final way that we make confrontation unnecessarily difficult is that we fail to show sufficient appreciation to co-workers. It is much easier for people to be receptive to the idea that some aspect of their performance needs to be improved if they believe that what they do is fully appreciated. If people do not feel appreciated at the time they begin a coaching session, they are already primed to respond negatively and uncooperatively during the discussion.

Test the following for yourself. Imagine that your manager or supervisor has indicated to you that he or she wants to discuss your performance with you tomorrow. What do you expect? You are in a very small minority if you expect your manager or supervisor to spend the time telling you what a good job you have been doing, that is, giving you *uncontaminated appreciation*.

Or consider the following: When a co-worker starts a conversation about our performance by telling us what a good job we have been doing, most of us fully expect "the other shoe to drop." We expect that our co-worker will finally get around to telling us what we are doing that he or she does not like.

Coaching does not exist in a vacuum. Its success depends on the kind of leadership practices that prevail in a work environment. This is particularly true of confrontation. We have a much greater chance to coach performance problems if we avoid criticizing, are timely in confronting performance problems, have established clear performance expectations, give and receive feedback that is timely and sufficient, and give regular and uncontaminated appreciation.

Coaching Process 2: Initiating Alternatives

Process Similarities

Compare Process 1: Responding to Needs (Exhibit 3.1), with Process 2: Initiating Alternatives (Exhibit 4.1), and you will note that they are similar in a number of ways:

- Both go through three interdependent stages.

- Stage II in both processes has essentially the same goals: information, insight, problem definition, and causes.

- Both processes employ many of the same skills—especially the general skills, such as acknowledging, probing, reflecting, and summarizing.

Process Differences

Both Process 1 and Process 2 flow through three stages from beginning to end. Both use all of the general skills identified with Process 1. Process 2 differs from Process 1 mainly in Stage I. In Process 1,

Exhibit 4.1. Coaching Process 2: Initiating Alternatives

Goals	Stage-Specific Skills	General Skills (typically useful at all stages)

Process Stage I: Stating Confrontation

Reduce resistance	*Confronting:* Making a statement that is specific, limited, and future oriented	*Attending:* Using nonverbal behavior to communicate and listening without evaluating
Limit topic		*Acknowledging:* Verbal and nonverbal indications of being involved in the conversation
Establish change focus		*Probing:* Asking questions and directing
		Reflecting: Stating in one's own words what the other person has said or is feeling
		Indicating respect: Not using behaviors that ridicule, generalize, or judge
		Self-disclosure: Indicating that one has had a similar experience
		Immediacy: Drawing attention to what is happening in the conversation
		Summarizing: Pausing in the conversation to summarize key points

Exhibit 4.1. *continued*

Goals	Stage-Specific Skills	General Skills (typically useful at all stages)

Process Stage II: Using Reaction to Develop Information

Goals	Stage-Specific Skills	General Skills
Defuse resistance	*Setting aside one's own agenda:* Mental discipline of focusing on what the other person needs to say and using the general skills to explore fully the other person's point of view	Attending
Insight		Acknowledging
		Probing
Problem definition/ causes		Reflecting
		Indicating respect
Causes		Self-disclosure
		Immediacy
		Summarizing

Process Stage III: Resolving

Goals	Stage-Specific Skills	General Skills
Ownership of problem or opportunity	*Reviewing:* Going over key points of session to ensure common understanding	Attending
		Acknowledging
Next steps		Probing
Commitment	*Planning:* Building strategies and agreeing on next steps	Reflecting
Positive relationship		Indicating respect
		Self-disclosure
Closure	*Affirming:* Commenting on a person's strengths and positive prospects	Immediacy
		Summarizing

either coaches or the persons being coached may initiate the conversation, but in Process 2, the conversation is initiated by the coach, who perceives the need for a change in performance. In Stage I of Process 2, the coach makes a confrontational statement. This beginning is quite different from Stage I in Process 1, where the coach is either responding to a need or presenting a perceived need.

Another difference is primarily a matter of emphasis. All successful coaching conversations conclude with the persons being coached taking the appropriate level of *ownership* for whatever needs to be learned or solved. Process 2 emphasizes ownership and makes it a specific goal during Stage III. At the start of the conversation the coach perceives that a problem exists. If the coach's perceptions are accurate and the conversation has been a success, the person being coached will accept his or her responsibility to resolve the problem or accept the opportunity presented by the coach.

Process Stage I: Stating Confrontation

Stage I Goals

A confrontation may be for the purpose of challenging people to accept an opportunity to take on tasks of greater responsibility or a confrontation may be for the purpose of correcting a performance problem. Stage I is typically quite brief in duration, consisting only of the coach's initial statement of what he or she wants to see fixed or improved. The goals of Stage I follow:

- To reduce resistance and negative emotions

- To limit the coaching topic

- To establish the change focus

Reduce Resistance

Reducing resistance and negative emotions is a more obvious goal in confrontations to correct a performance problem than it is in confrontations that challenge people to accept an opportunity to do more responsible or difficult work. It is critically important when confronting unsatisfactory performance.

Successful coaches do not confront others about their performance to make them angry, upset, irritated, or depressed. They confront in order to change performance. They do not set out to stimulate negative emotions in others. But, in spite of how disciplined and skilled we are in confronting others, some level of negative emotion will be typically generated. Knowing how to use the negative reactions of others is the mark of a skilled coach.

Limit the Coaching Topic

A second goal of Stage I is for coaches to limit or establish initial boundaries of the problem that they wish to discuss. Being clear about this goal and focusing on it helps reduce negative reactions. The more indefinite a confrontation is or the greater the number of separate issues that it includes, the more intense will be the other person's reactions.

We cannot, of course, predict what the final content of a coaching conversation will be. The coach may start out perceiving the problem to be X. But during the conversation it may become apparent that the problem is really Z. Still, whatever the final problem turns out to be, it is most efficient for the coach to start with the clearest possible delineation of one specific problem. Only in this way can both coach and the persons being coached reach agreement as quickly as possible about the precise nature of the problem.

When coaches are dealing with a problem in performance, not challenging a person to higher levels of performance, they often have considerable difficulty limiting the topic for the following reasons:

1. They have avoided timely confrontation and let performance problems accumulate.

2. They are unclear in their own minds about what they want to discuss because they have never clarified performance standards.

3. They really want to talk about one issue, but they are uncomfortable talking about it so they start with a less threatening issue.

The first two reasons were discussed above. The third reason, talking about one thing when we really want to talk about another, requires an illustration:

. . . .

A president of a large consulting firm for whom I was doing some work had a vice president who continually antagonized most of the other vice presidents and senior executives by insisting on his own way whenever any issues arose about budgets and resources. When the president finally got around to confronting the vice president, he began the conversation like this: "I'd like for you to take the initiative with our strategic planning this time around. It will give you a chance to get to know the other senior staff better. How are you getting along with them, by the way?" Of course, the problem that he really wanted to talk about was his perception of the vice president's lack of cooperation with his peers. He never got to the real problem.

. . . .

Coaches can only hope to fix the performance problem they discuss. To conduct an effective and efficient confrontation, coaches must state up front exactly what it is that they perceive to be the problem.

Establish Change Focus

All successful coaching conversations are oriented toward change. This focus is critical for confrontation and is an explicit goal in Stage I of Process 1.

Coaches must communicate at the outset of the coaching conversation that they want to fix a concrete and specifically defined performance. It is critical to the success of the whole coaching process that the coaches indicate that they are interested in what can be done in the future, not in what has occurred in the past. This does not mean that the past is not important and that a discussion of causes for a problem should not occur. It means only that the coach must create an environment for the conversation that implicitly says: "I want to fix what is wrong, not blame you for what is wrong."

Establishing a change focus, like limiting the problem, also tends to reduce negative reactions. It is much less threatening for a person to talk about what can be fixed (the future) than it is for a person to talk about what cannot be fixed (the past).

Stage I Skills

Stage I consists of establishing exactly what the coach wants to talk about. The skill required is the ability to make a useful statement of the problem (in the case of confronting a performance problem) or to describe briefly the new job or career opportunity (in the case of challenging people to accept greater responsibility). The one skill required is the stage-specific skill of phrasing the issue. The most useful confrontations are specific, limit the problem, and are future oriented.

Be Specific

Being specific refers to the coach's stating precisely what the performance expectation is and how the other person's performance has differed from the expectation. A good rule of thumb is this: *If we cannot describe exactly what we want to be different, then there is no point in confronting someone about his or her performance.*

The following confrontations illustrate the characteristic of being specific:

- "I believe that we all agreed that every team member would be at the training sessions on the new software. I have been to every session and I haven't seen the whole team there once."

- "The travel office has informed us on several occasions that, unless there is an emergency, travel requests must be submitted at least forty-eight hours prior to actual travel. I have three memos here from the travel office that indicate you have not been following the rule."

Limit the Problem

When phrasing a confrontation about a performance problem, it is important to limit the initial confrontation made in Stage I to a single problem, even if there are several problems that should be addressed. Further, the confrontation should start with the most recent example of the performance problem.

When some of us get around to a coaching session with co-workers, we may have saved up a number of problems and begin our confrontation something like this:

> There have been numerous instances over the past couple of months when you have been late with your input for the team's weekly report that I put together. And even when you have given your data to me on time, it consists of notes that I have had to rewrite. If that were not enough, you have even complained to me that you didn't think I always gave your information sufficient space in the report.

A more effective style for this coach would be to begin with the most recent example of one problem and fix that problem. If there were time, the coach could go on to another problem. It is, of course, highly likely that the other related problems would surface during the conversation and the coach could propose an orderly way of managing them. In the example above, the coach might begin with: "You didn't give me your input for the weekly report on time last week. I can't do my job without your input. What can we do about the problem?"

When coaches wait to confront co-workers about problems that have persisted over some period of time, they are often tempted to start their confrontation by describing the general problem, rather than starting with the most recent example of the problem. Take for example a person who continues to be late for team meetings. The team leader may start with a confrontation such as: "You haven't been coming to meetings on time." It would be more efficient for the coach to start by limiting the problem to the most recent example of the team member's performance: "You were about fifteen minutes late at our team's morning status meeting."

Confusion, resistance, and negative emotions tend to be limited and the overall efficiency of the coaching session increased if the coach and person being coached quickly agree on a concrete point of reference. Limiting the problem in the confrontation helps to establish this point.

Be Future Oriented

Another characteristic of useful confrontations is that they are future oriented. Compare the examples below, which contrast being future oriented with being past oriented:

> *Past Oriented:* "I need all members of the project team present on time at our weekly status review. Why have you missed two out of the last three meetings?"

> *Future Oriented:* "I need all members of the project present on time at our weekly status review. What can you do to make sure that you don't miss these meetings?"

Past Oriented: "You missed our last budget submission cutoff date by two days. What seems to be the problem?"

Future Oriented: "You missed our last budget submission cutoff date by two days. What can you do to make sure you hit the date in the future?"

Being specific, limiting the problem, and being future oriented will contribute directly to brief confrontations. Once presented with a clear definition of the problem and the coach's explicitly stated desire to fix it, the person being coached will often acknowledge the legitimacy of the coach's confrontation and indicate what he or she intends to do about it. In terms of Process 2, the conversation goes directly from Stage I to Stage III. Let me illustrate:

COACH: The error rate on your machine was above limits yesterday. What are you doing to bring it down within limits?

OTHER: I found a calibration problem in the input chute. I was accepting material that was outside limits, but I've got the problem licked and I'm back to normal.

COACH: Thanks for staying on top of it. Let me know if you run into the problem again. We may have to put a bit more pressure on the supplier.

Put the Skills Together

Stage I covers only the initial presentation or confrontation in Process 2. Stage I is a statement designed to achieve the following goals:

- Reduce resistance and negative emotions

- Limit the performance topic

- Establish a change focus

Reaching these goals is greatly assisted if the confrontation is specific, limits the problem or opportunity, and is future oriented. The following are complete examples of Stage I statements that have all three characteristics:

- "As scheduling clerk, you know I'm responsible for keeping current data on milestones and updating the schedule each week. In our last team meeting you really surprised me with the news that your last shipment of resisters was below standard and you would have to slip schedule for at least two weeks. What can we do to ensure that I hear that kind of news immediately in the future?"

- "Our service team set the standard of developing not just satisfied customers, but outrageously satisfied and enthusiastic customers. Here it is Monday and we have six complaints from our customers that they requested help over the weekend and couldn't get it. We can't keep our standard and have this sort of thing happening. What do you all think we should do to fix this problem?"

- "Tidewater Shipping says that you didn't complete the asbestos removal job. They say we failed to strip the asbestos from the pipes in their generator room. Let's first talk about fixing Tidewater's problem and then about what you can do to keep this sort of thing from happening again."

Process Stage II:
Using Reaction to Develop Information

The most difficult part of Process 2 occurs during Stage II. This stage of the process requires more discipline than any other element in coaching. When people are confronted about a performance problem they can be expected to react. Unskilled coaches will respond in one or more of the following ways to the reactions from the persons being coached.

If the persons being coached make excuses or give reasons for the problem, unskilled coaches will

- Dismiss or refute the other person's excuses or reasons for the problem

- Respond to the other person's excuses or reasons by restating the confrontation

- Aggravate the negative impact of the confrontation by quoting policy or giving some other kind of argument

If the persons being coached take the offensive and begin to attack, unskilled coaches will

- React to their aggressive behavior by becoming more aggressive themselves

- Retreat and back off from the confrontation

The guiding principle in confronting a performance problem is, *Don't fight the person's reaction; fix the performance problem.*

Stage II Goals

The goals in Stage II parallel those of Stage II in Process 1: information, insight, and definition of the problem or opportunity. However, there is an additional goal: defusing resistance.

Each time coaches confront co-workers, they introduce the possibility of change. Each time they introduce change, they introduce the possibility of resistance. Initiating alternatives requires that coaches accept the responsibility for managing the resistance that they have created. One major step in managing resistance is to dissipate the negative emotions associated with resistance. Think of the process this way. By encouraging others to explore their opinions, feelings, points of view, reasons, and excuses, coaches are helping them transform negative feelings into verbal behavior and to become less and less negative.

During Stage II, the skilled coach develops all the information that is needed for both coach and the person coached to understand the problem or opportunity being discussed, to gain insight into one another's points of view, and to determine what should be changed. In cases of performance problems, it is the problem itself and its causes that must be accurately defined. In the case of a performance opportunity, it is the opportunity that must be explored and understood.

The accurate definition of a performance problem and its causes also takes place during Stage II. Confrontation starts with what the coach knows, but a successful coaching conversation develops what both coach and the person coached know. Coaches start a confrontation session with their own points of view—opinions about a performance problem or a performance opportunity—but there is always the possibility that the coach's perception is not accurate. By stimulating and encouraging co-workers to explore issues and causes from their own points of view, coaches may discover that the problem is something quite different.

I have described Coaching Process 1 as a linear process so that the process could be easily understood and become a model for practice and learning. In actual practice, confrontation is a cyclical and iterative process (Figure 4.2). In the case of confrontation, it is often this cyclical and iterative quality that contributes to the process's success. Let me illustrate this cyclical and iterative quality in the case of a performance problem:

- *Stage I.* The person is confronted with the coach's perception of the performance problem.

- *Stage II.* The person being confronted reacts to the confrontation—usually by giving reasons and causes for

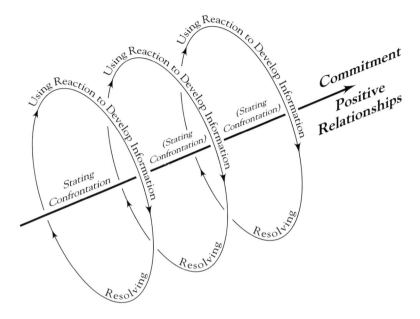

Figure 4.2. The Cyclical Nature of Coaching Process 2

the problem. The coach sets aside his or her own agenda and uses the other person's reaction to gather information and develop a mutual understanding of the problem. Two things can occur at this point: (1) no new information can come out, so the performance problem remains as the coach initially perceived it, or (2) new information is brought out and the coach modifies his or her perception.

- *Return to Stage I.* If no new understanding is developed, then the coach returns to Stage I and repeats the initial confrontation. If a new understanding is developed, then the coach returns to Stage I, but modifies the confrontation to fit his or her new perception of the problem. Process 2 has begun a second iteration.

- *Return to Stage II and further iterations.* Once Stage I is repeated, Process 2 has begun a second iteration. These iterations will be repeated so long as the problem definition is modified and until the coach and the person being coached have accurately identified the problem that has first priority for resolution.

Stage II Skills

All of the general skills described in Process I come into play in reaching the goals of Stage II of Process 2: attending, acknowledging, showing respect, probing, etc. These are the skills for using the reaction to a confrontation to develop information. In both processes, Stage II is fully focused on the needs of the persons being coached. The one stage-specific skill for Stage II in Process 2 is the mental skill of setting aside one's own agenda.

Setting aside one's agenda does not mean that the coach forgets all about the problem or opportunity as phrased in Stage I. But coaches cannot focus on the other person and fully explore the other person's reactions and point of view unless they can mentally "let go" of their own definition of the problem or opportunity.

I have found in the coaching workshops that I have conducted that participants are not all that comfortable with the notion of setting aside their own agendas as they practice the skills of Process 2. Of course, I am not suggesting that coaches forget why they started a conversation, but only by responding directly and fully to what the other person says in reaction to a confrontation can they find out enough information to solve the performance problem or resolve questions about new job responsibilities. It is by helping the other persons explore fully their reactions to our confrontations that we can turn the confrontations into problem-solving conversation—ones that are mutual and in which the other persons are fully involved and feel fully respected.

Coaches can redirect a conversation back to their original agenda at any time. It is not possible, however, to progress through

Stage II unless the other persons are given the freedom to present their points of view and explore their feelings. Setting aside our agenda permits us to move into Stage III and develop the information we need to understand and fix the problem.

Shown below are two examples of what setting aside one's agenda looks like after a confrontation has been made:

CONFRONTATION: I tried to call the office three times this morning from the field station, and all I got was the answering service. When I am in the field talking to our customers, I badly need to be able to reach this office and talk to a person and get a quick response. Have you got any ideas?

RESPONSE: I can't do everything. I have to leave my desk sometimes, and there isn't anyone else around to cover for me.

NOT SETTING ASIDE: I'm sure that there are a lot of excuses for not covering the phones, but I must insist that they be covered.

SETTING ASIDE: Why don't we start by listing all the problems that you are having, and then see what kind of solutions are most feasible? (open probe)

CONFRONTATION: I don't have your submission to our team's budget yet. I thought the team had established yesterday as the deadline. I have to have the draft in by Wednesday for the director's approval. When can you get your part to me?

REACTION: I'm really sorry; it's just that I've had so many crises develop this week. I guess I'll have to drop everything else and get on the budget.

NOT SETTING ASIDE: Being sorry doesn't do much good right now. You've put the whole team in a very difficult position. I must have your input immediately.

SETTING ASIDE: Sounds like you have had to manage a lot of unexpected problems. (reflecting)

Process Stage III: Resolving

Goals of Stage III

The general and overarching goals of all coaching conversations are to obtain commitment to higher levels of performance, while maintaining positive work relationships between coach and the persons coached. As with Coaching Process 1, it is the careful progress through each of the stages in Process 2 that leads to these goals. No single comment during a coaching conversation leads to reaching these goals. It is by the character and quality of the entire conversation that we reach them. Commitment is built throughout the conversation as coaches clarify goals and values, improve people's competency, extend the influence of co-workers, and express appreciation to them for their achievements. Positive relationships are developed, maintained, and strengthened by coaches adhering to the fundamental characteristics of successful coaching, that is, by communicating respect, ensuring that the conversation is mutual, focusing on the problem, and staying future oriented. In addition to the general goals of commitment and positive relationships, Stage III has the specific goals of ownership, next steps, and closure.

Ownership

Ownership describes the other person's expressed willingness to assume his or her appropriate responsibility for fixing the problem or for planning to take advantage of a new job opportunity.

In the case of performance problems, people may indicate *explicit* ownership of a problem and say something such as: "I recognize that I should have checked these priorities out with you before I assumed which ones were most important." But people may indicate *implicit* ownership by describing what they are going to do to fix a problem. Thus: "I'll turn in the budget to you by the end of the day." It is not important that people explicitly state that they have created a problem. What is important is that they state how they are going to fix a problem.

A fundamental principle of improving the performance of others is to make it as easy as possible for people to improve. It is often easier for people to accept responsibility for fixing performance problems than it is for them to admit that they have made a mistake or failed in some way. In confronting performance problems, it is well to recognize that ownership has occurred when people give a clear signal that they are going to fix the performance problem—even if they never explicitly say that they are responsible for the problem in the first place.

Next Steps

Next steps is a goal in Process 1, but it is a goal that must be *emphasized* in Process 2. The best coaching sessions to improve performance or raise performance to a higher level include some discussion of "next steps." This means identifying specific strategies for resolving the problem and both coach and the person coached agreeing on the steps to be taken. Included in the next steps should be some provision for keeping the coach informed of the other person's progress. Here are two examples:

- "I will get right on the budget submission, and I'll let you know immediately if I still run into problems that will keep me from meeting the new deadline."

- "The first thing I am going to do is review the contract provisions with the supplier. I'll let the team know if that doesn't solve our problem of noncompliance."

Closure

Closure is the goal of ensuring that the persons being coached have a sense of completeness. In the case of performance problems, this means that they feel they have been fully heard and that they have identified exactly what they can do to fix the problem. They are not left with the feeling that they must manage some intangible or vague problem like "being more professional," "being a better team player," "or being more diligent." A sense of closure is ensured by reviewing what has transpired during the coaching conversation and by affirming the other person's strengths.

Stage III Skills

Stage III of Process 2 has the same stage-specific skills as Stage III in Process 1: reviewing, planning, and affirming. The skills are the same in both processes, but it is well to look at some examples of how these skills look for Process 2.

Reviewing

Reviewing has particular importance when the confrontation has been occasioned by a performance problem. Reviewing ensures clarity at the end of a conversation during which quite different points of view may have emerged. Reviewing helps achieve the goal of closure. It also encourages a demonstration of the other person's commitment. The following are some examples of what reviewing might sound like in a performance improvement session:

- "I started this conversation by asking you about the technical review that our client has been requesting. My understanding had been that we had agreed that you were giving it priority treatment. We seem to have misunderstood each other about that, so you have been giving time to other projects and felt it was all right to delay the review. Also, you indicated that you were running into problems with the data analysis branch and not receiving a timely response from that group. We've clarified the matter of just how important the review is. What we need to do now is figure out what has to be done to get a better response on the data analysis and how we can finish the review just as soon as possible."

- "I guess we got off on a pretty rocky start with this conversation. I had my point of view and you had yours about what is happening as we change to this new team concept for customer service. I think, however, that we've agreed on the basic issue: we can't spend the time we need to develop our service team and still have time to give our customers what they want. What we need to do now is figure out a plan that will get our team up and running without damaging our customer relations."

Here is what reviewing might sound like in a conversation in which a co-worker has been confronted with an opportunity to take on more responsibility:

- "I think you know how important it is to take advantage of these new opportunities that are developing because of the Internet. I'm glad that I understand better your reservations about moving into our web page department. Most of all, I'm glad that you haven't turned down the opportunity and are ready to do some research before we talk about this again."

Planning

When coaching people about improving their performance or accepting new job opportunities, planning is the skill that identifies next steps—the strategies to follow to resolve the problem or take advantage of the opportunity and a way to keep the coach informed of progress. Some coaches do a very credible job of confronting only to lose the payoff because they do not give sufficient attention to planning. Planning does not mean that the persons coached merely indicate that they will correct a problem or think about an opportunity. Voiced intentions to correct a problem or think about an opportunity for more responsibility have limited value.

Skilled coaches will develop with the persons coached a set of specific actions to solve the problem or take advantage of the chance for greater responsibility. They will assist in planning the next steps. The following are examples of planning statements:

- "Get back to me on Monday and give me your ideas on what we can do to help you be more involved with the design shop so we can avoid the kind of conflict that seems to develop when your fabrication shop receives a design."

- "Okay, so you'll talk to the people in the customer service office, find out more of the specific things they do, decide if you want to make the move, and get back to me within a week."

Affirming

People who have been involved in a performance improvement coaching interaction can easily leave the session with some unresolved negative feelings. But people who have been confronted with the possibility of taking on a more demanding job can also leave a coaching session feeling uncertain and confused about what they want to do. It is important that coaches end a confrontation with some positive comments about the other person's strengths, the general strengths that persons have exhibited in their jobs as well as the efforts that they have made *during* the coaching interaction. The goal, of course, is to leave others with positive belief in themselves and their capacity to succeed. Here are some examples of what affirming can sound like at the end of a conversation to improve performance:

- "I know that this conversation has been tough for you, but you have been very candid and forthright in describing how we got ourselves into this difficulty. I have no doubt that you can fix the problem and keep it from happening again."

- "It has always been clear to me that you care a great deal about keeping the people in purchasing happy. Your proposal to have weekly status meetings with them should solve the problem."

Here is an example of what affirming might look like in the case of confronting a person about a new job opportunity:

- "You've already shown that you have the skills to take the lead in our next research project, and I know that you have more knowledge of how to design surveys than nearly anyone else around. We'll be appointing a lead next week, and I would sure hate to see you miss out."

The next sections in this chapter present two examples of confronting. In the first example, the coach is confronting a person to take on a more demanding job. In the second example, the coach is confronting a person to fix a performance problem.

Examples of Coaching Process 2: Initiating Alternatives

In the examples that follow, C is the symbol used for coach. O stands for the other person, the one being coached. The person doing the coaching can be anyone who wants to take on this function and is permitted to do so.

The left-hand column records a coaching conversation. In the right-hand column, I have identified the stages and skills of the process. Not all the skills are illustrated in each example—just as not all skills would always be used in any specific coaching conversation.

How to Use the Examples

The examples illustrate the goals, stages, and skills for Coaching Process 2 for both challenging a person to assume more responsibility and for confronting a person because of performance that must be improved. These examples can be powerful learning tools for you and help you transfer your learning to on-the-job applications of effective and efficient coaching practices, if you will do the following:

1. Before you read through an example, review Process 2—the stages, goals, general skills, and stage-specific skills in Exhibit 4.1.

2. Cover up the right-hand column of the examples and test your own ability to identify the stages and skills.

3. After you have gone through an example once, read through it again and substitute your own responses.

Example 1: Challenging a Person to Accept a More Complex Job

Challenging Conversation	Comments
C: Mark, you've been the manager for our project management training program for a year now	*Stage I: Stating Confrontation*
I've always had in mind that you would begin to take more direct responsibility for delivering some of the modules. Right now we are under pressure to reduce the cost that goes for outside trainers. I'd like to see you begin to deliver some of the content modules.	Confronting
O: I think I would like to do that, but I'm not sure it would work.	

We've been using trainers who have strong reputations for being authorities in their particular areas. I'm not sure I would have the acceptance or credibility they do.

C: So you would like to start delivering some of the modules, and I guess that means you feel you have the content in hand; it's the matter of acceptance that bothers you and gives you some concern.

Stage II: Using Reaction to Develop Information

Dropping agenda
Reflecting

O: That's right.

C: You seem willing to take on the job of delivering some modules, so I guess what we need to work on is your concern about being accepted. What ideas do you have that could help establish your credibility?

Stage III: Resolving

Open probe

O: I can think of several. First, I would like to get more experience working in projects. I've been on plenty of project teams, but I really need to manage one. Second, I would like to co-train with some of our outside experts and get some reputation for doing the up-front stuff. Also, I would like to have a chance to deliver some sessions away from the company, where questions about my credibility won't matter as much.

C: All of those are good ideas, and I think we can work on them in

Acknowledging

parallel. We need to revise some of
our large training programs. One
that comes to mind is our residential
executive program. That can be your
project, if you want it. So we're
agreed that you will get ready as
soon as possible to deliver some of
the content in the project management program and that you'll use
your ideas. How about working up
a plan to start delivering some of
the content modules as soon as possible? You can build into it all the
things you want to do to make you
more comfortable in the job. I
don't have any doubt that you can
do the job, and I think you are
doing exactly what's needed to get
ready. How about going over the
plan with me in a week?

Resourcing

Reviewing

Planning

Affirming

Planning

O: Okay, I'll see you in a week.

Example 2: Confronting Unsuccessful Performance

Confrontational Conversation	*Comments*
C: Thanks for coming in, Nate. I know how busy you are and I wouldn't be taking up your time except that I have a problem that we need to fix. It seems that your crew has accumulated a real backlog of maintenance requests, and I really got an earful of complaints from some	*Stage I: Stating Confrontation*
	Confronting

department heads this morning at our session with the director. People are complaining to their department heads and are making the case that we just are not being as responsive as people expect in completing the repairs that are requested. All of the complaints are focused on your sector. I would like for us to figure out what kind of a problem we have and then figure out just what we must do to keep our customers satisfied. I sure don't want to go through another meeting like I did this morning.

O: I guess people don't believe in acts of God anymore. That last Northeaster that hit us created a real mess. We've been swamped with requests for repairing water damage and fixing roofs. Our work force was cut 15 percent at the beginning of the year, and people still expect the same level of service. Even without the Northeaster we would have a backlog of requests.

Person reacts, defending self and providing more information

C: So, you see the problem being that you're understaffed and then we got hit by the storm that created a real overload.

Stage II: Using Reaction to Develop Information

Reflecting

O: That's about it. I think we have a problem of unreasonable expectations. Most of the people around here still think we're living in the days when we could hire just about whomever we needed. They haven't adjusted to the fact that times have changed. I'm certainly aware that some people are unhappy, but frankly I think we're doing about the best we can with what we have.

C: You see unreasonable expectations figuring into the problem also. What do you make of the fact that the teams assigned to the other three sectors don't seem to be having the problem that you're having?

Reflecting

Open probe

O: I would like to say "luck," but I know that's not the case. Maybe the other teams just have better people. I don't know; maybe it's me. It sure looks like the other sectors are not having the same kind of problem that I'm having.

C: People may be part of the problem. I have no reason to believe that you're not qualified for the job. How about focusing on the idea that the other sectors are not having your problem and seeing if we can come up with some ways to fix the problem of these complaints?

Acknowledging

Affirming

Stage III: Resolving
Open probe

O: Okay by me.

C: Let me test with you a couple of things that I know the other sector

Resourcing

teams are doing. I know that they stay really close to their customers. Once they take a job order, they make a specific person responsible for that customer and the customer's order. They give the customer a progress report so that the customer always knows the status of the job—how far along to completion and any anticipated delays. They also do something else. They review their backlogs at the end of each week and figure out how they can clear them out. Sometimes they can clear them out. Sometimes they will contact one customer and agree on a later completion so they can put their efforts into cleaning up three or four other jobs that are not so complex. There are some other things that they do—things I don't even know about. But this is enough to test with you whether you are doing the same sort of things.

Open probe

O: I can't say that we are all that systematic, but I think we try to keep our customers informed. But then maybe we should do more. I know people don't complain as much if they are kept aware of what's going on.

C: What do you think about getting with the other sector leaders and finding out at least two things: one,

Planning

what steps they take to keep from accumulating too big a backlog of work orders, and two, what they do to stay in touch with their customers and keep them happy.

O: I'll do it, but it looks like I don't know what I'm doing and have to go around begging for help.

C: I've found it difficult at times to ask others for help, but most of the time it's paid off. Would you like to try other ways to solve the problems of backlog and customer complaints?

Self-disclosure

Planning
Closed probe

O: I would like to work with my team on the problem and get them involved in contacting the other sector teams and finding out what might work with us. Give me a week and let me come up with a plan for fixing the problem. More than that, give me a week to do something about the problem and show you what we are planning to do.

C: I can wait a week. Am I right in expecting you to show improvement in the backlog problem and to put a plan together to keep the backlog under control and to make your customers happy.

Planning
Reviewing
Open probe

O: Right, I'll see you a week from today.

Planning

Key Learning Points for Chapter Four

1. Confronting is a positive process and should not be confused with criticizing.

2. Confrontation includes those conversations that focus on encouraging persons to take on greater responsibility as well as those that address performance problems.

3. Confrontation of performance problems is often made more difficult than it needs to be because coaches

   - Do not establish clear performance standards
   - Do not create sufficient and timely performance feedback
   - Do not express enough appreciation to people for their contributions

4. Process 1 and Process 2 have these important similarities:

   - Both go through three interdependent stages.
   - Stage II in both processes has essentially the same goals.
   - Both processes employ the same general skills.

5. Process 1 and Process 2 differ in the following ways:

   - In Process 1, either the coach or the other person may initiate the conversation, but in Process 2 the conversation is initiated by the coach who perceives the job opportunity or performance problem.
   - Because Stage I in Process 2 begins with a confrontational statement, this process most often stimulates stronger resistance from the other person than is the case in Process 1.
   - Ownership is emphasized in Process 2 more than in Process 1. Confrontation begins with a problem or opportunity that a coach perceives to exist. A major goal of confrontation is to transfer appropriate responsibility from the coach to the persons being coached—or at least to develop a sense of shared responsibility.

6. Coaching Process 2: Initiating Alternatives has the following stages and goals:

- Stage I: Confronting or Presenting

  - Reduce resistance
  - Limit the topic
  - Establish change focus

- Stage II: Using Reaction to Develop Information

  - Defuse resistance
  - Develop information
  - Agree on problem
  - Identify causes

- Stage III: Resolving

  - Ownership of problem
  - Next steps
  - Positive relationship
  - Commitment
  - Closure

5

Coaching Teams

Everyone has opportunities to coach, and the overall performance of organizations is improved when more and more people assume that responsibility. Coaching is not a function limited to people with assigned leadership roles. This becomes especially obvious when we look at teams.

On high-performing teams, we typically find that the leadership role moves easily from one member to another. Each time members take the initiative to help their team learn, solve problems, improve meetings, set goals, plan performance strategies, or perform any performance task, they act as leaders. The more teams become self-managed, the more obvious it becomes that leadership must be a shared responsibility. In high-performing teams, leadership is usually exercised by anyone who can help the team perform at its full potential. The practical meaning of this is that members of the best teams are always helping the team and other individuals on the team learn and solve problems—that is, *they coach.*

The successful coaching of teams includes all of the functions that are associated with one-on-one coaching: counseling, mentoring, tutoring, challenging, and confronting. It also requires all the competencies included in the two coaching processes. But coaching more than one person at a time, as is the case when coaching teams, requires some additional understanding and skills. Coaching teams also requires a knowledge of the factors that influence the way groups communicate and do business when they meet.

Team coaching obviously happens when two or more members are together. It takes place when most members of a team are meeting. Team coaches are not interacting with just one other person, but with the whole team. Team coaching requires at least three sets of skills in addition to the ones covered in previous chapters. It requires: (1) that coaches have knowledge and skills to help teams structure themselves for effective team meetings; (2) that coaches have the knowledge and skills to manage interactions among team members and between team members and themselves; and (3) that coaches are skilled in the basics of team problem solving and decision making.

Knowledge and Skills to Help Teams Structure Themselves for Effective Team Meetings

Two of the most obvious and effective practices in structuring a team are the following:

- Ensure that the team develops and uses a clear set of norms that govern how members interact

- Ensure that the team is always clear and conscious of its tasks and goals

Developing and Using Norms

Structure describes everything that a team does to determine what is expected of team members during a meeting. Structuring a team does not mean setting up the sorts of rules that one might use in large meetings or with groups that are not teams. The success of team meetings depends on maintaining a balance between freedom and control. Structuring a team meeting means helping a team conduct its meetings in a purposeful, rational, and fully conscious manner—while making full use of the mental resources of all team members. Structuring a team should never mean avoiding disagreement or conflict. The most creative results of teams are often produced by playing alternatives against one another.

Norms are listed first, not because norms are more important than tasks, objectives, and goals, but because teams that are not clear about what they intend to do can never be teams in fact. They remain groups of people, but they can never be teams. Teams always perform real work, and superior teams are always quite clear what this work is. Having norms helps raise the potential of teams by strengthening their capacity to perform their tasks and reach their objectives and goals.

Norms set explicit expectations about the behavior of team members before, during, and after a meeting. Norms largely accomplish two things. They (1) set responsibilities and (2) establish communication standards.

To ensure that norms affect team performance, they must be written. Until they have become second nature for members, they should also be visible during meetings, displayed on a flip chart or in some other way.

Norms communicate at the beginning of a team meeting explicitly what is expected. During and at the end of a meeting they provide the basis for teams to evaluate their performance and to adjust it, if needed. During their early days of development, it is good practice for teams to review their norms at the start of each meeting.

It will soon become apparent to anyone who understands the basics of team coaching whether teams have clear and explicit norms. Teams that do not will exhibit the following kinds of problems:

- Not everyone will be present at the start of a meeting.

- Meetings will not start or end on time.

- Members will not be properly prepared for a meeting.

- Some members will not remain present during the whole meeting.

- Some members will not be fully involved during a meeting.

- The team will not stay focused on what it started out to do and will stray from its tasks.

- Members will often be unsure of exactly what the team is doing.

- Proper records of meetings will not be kept.

- One or two members will often dominate the meeting.

- It will not be clear at the outset of a discussion just how a decision will be made, whether by vote, leader's authority, or consensus.

Most of these problems occur when teams fail to set and enforce norms around responsibilities and communication standards. Norms that set responsibilities may include the following:

- Meetings will start and end on time.

- The role of meeting leader will rotate among members.

- Decisions reached by the team will be recorded and published to team members.

- No member will leave a meeting while it is in progress.

- All decisions will be made by consensus.

Norms that set expectations about communication might state that each team member will

- Listen and make sure that he or she has understood what other members mean before speaking

- Pay careful attention to how much each person talks and ensure that there is a balanced interaction among members

- Never discount or ridicule what other members say

- Consistently speak to the task the team is performing

- Summarize periodically what has been said during a meeting

- Help others make a contribution

- Be candid and always express his or her own mind and opinion

- Be concrete and factual

Norms that effectively structure how team meetings are conducted must always represent the whole team so that the norms are managed by the team and reinforced by the team. This means that the norms must be developed by consensus and that they must be regularly reviewed and modified by consensus.

Helping teams establish norms for their meetings, helping them actively use the norms to structure their meetings, helping them use the norms in real time to adjust team performance, and helping them use their norms to assess their performance can all be intended outcomes of team coaching.

If teams do not have norms, the first object of coaching is to help the team recognize the practical importance of norms and their utility. The kind of interventions that a team coach might make to help a team set norms will sound like the following:

- "We are losing a lot of information because some of us are talking at the same time and we are not listening to each other as well as we might. I would like for us to set some guidelines about the way we expect to communicate when we meet."

- "I'm not clear about what we expect of each other before our team meetings or after the meetings. I would like to see us set some ground rules that help all of us remember what we are supposed to do."

- "We seem to be letting the leadership of the team fall to anyone who takes over. I think we ought to make a conscious decision about it. Do we appoint a leader for some period? Do we not want to have an appointed leader? Do we want to rotate leadership from meeting to meeting? Besides that, what do we expect of a person who is acting as leader?"

If teams have set their norms but during a meeting are not adhering to these norms, coach might intervene in one of the following ways:

- "We have a norm that states that no person will monopolize the conversation. It seems to me that is exactly what has been happening for the last fifteen minutes."

- "We've started this meeting without doing what we set as a norm. We haven't reviewed the outcomes that we expect to achieve."

- "I'm looking at the norm that we agreed to that says no one will leave our meetings while they are in progress. We've had three members leave since we started. What do we want to do about it?"

Tasks, Objectives, and Goals

A second condition that affects a team's structure during a meeting is whether the team is clear about what it is doing and what it intends to produce. Clarifying what a team is doing and what it intends to accomplish does not mean that a team will not go off course. If, however, members keep before the team what it is doing and what it has set out to do, the team stays conscious of its goals, so that if it deviates from those goals, it does so by conscious choice.

The key word here is *conscious*. Teams, like individuals, can become quite unconscious about what they are doing at any one time. One factor in structuring teams is that members be clear about their tasks, objectives, and goals. But structuring teams also means keeping members continuously aware of what they are doing, that is, conscious of their performance. When persons take the initiative to coach a team and bring it back on track, they might say something like the following:

- "When we started this meeting we agreed that we would make a decision about how we would manage our travel funds. We seem to have gotten off on another subject. I suggest we decide now whether we want to work on the travel funds problem and decide how we will manage the funds or whether we want to leave that subject and work on some other problem."

- "We set up this meeting to decide how we would measure our team's performance. For the past ten minutes we have been debating whether or not our performance could be measured. I suggest that we settle what we are here to do. Are we here to establish a set of measures, or are we here to debate whether or not we can measure our performance?"

Knowledge and Skills to Manage Interactions Among Team Members and with Oneself

The first type of special knowledge and skills that coaches of teams require is to understand that teams must have structure, what teams must do to build structure, and how to help them build structure. A second type of special knowledge and skills that team coaches must have is the competency to manage the interactions among team members and the interactions of team members with the coach.

Managing communication during a coaching session with a team begins, of course, with mastery of the two processes and skills already described. Communicating with a team, however, requires additional knowledge about how to interact with more than one person at a time. The special competencies required include the following:

- Helping team members build on one another's input

- Testing to ensure understanding

- Keeping all members involved

Building on One Another's Input

When teams are not sufficiently disciplined during meetings, they will often not take into account what each member says and fail to develop information systematically, thus not using the full resources of the team. Member A will say something, Member B will ignore what Member A said and make a comment, Member C will ignore what both A and B said and give input, and so on. As the team continues in its interaction, what A, B, C, and other members have said will be forgotten and go unused. In the example that follows, the coach is trying to help a computer service team select the best measures of its performance. Team members (X, Y, Z) give input, which is ignored. The coach (C) intervenes to help the team build on the input of its members and not ignore the input.

> X: We need measures that really mean something. Just counting how many software packages we test or how many computers we repair will turn us into bean counters.
> Y: I think its management's job to tell us what to measure. The managers know what kind of information they want, so we should just go back and ask them.

C: X has indicated that he wants to make sure our measures are really meaningful. Y says we ought to let management decide what we should measure. We need to discuss both of those ideas, but maybe what Y said needs to be discussed first. If we think we can go back to management to tell us what to measure, then we will need to decide just how to this.

Z: There is no way we can go back to management. We would look really stupid. Besides, I don't want somebody else telling us what to measure. I want our team to control as much as we can what we do.

Y: I think what I said was a bit of wishful thinking. We need to do this ourselves.

C: Okay, if you are all together on this, let's start with the question of how we can make sure that we measure our performance in a way that makes sense.

Testing to Ensure Understanding

Coaches can test for understanding at any point in a team's process by phrasing in their own words what they think the team has done up to that point, or coaches may ask team members to restate in their own words what has just been said or summarize what has been covered up to some point in the meeting. Another way to test for understanding is for coaches to give examples to illustrate some point or concept or to ask someone else to give examples.

Coaches can also test for understanding by making connections among the inputs made or helping team members make such connections. Inputs that a coach might make would sound like the following:

- "If the team decides to measure and reduce the costs to deliver a service call, how will that impact customer satisfaction?"

- "We've decided to develop operating procedures for our service team. That's going to take time. How will we be

able to maintain our current levels of service if we have
to spend so much time organizing ourselves?"

- "We've identified at least three causes for the delay
  in response time. Do you think that these causes
  are all different, or do they all come down to the same
  thing?"

Keeping All Members Involved

Coaching a team means coaching *all* the members of a team.
Involvement is not merely desirable socially but is absolutely necessary for the team to do its best work. For team learning to take
place, every team member must learn what is required. For a team
to solve a problem and use all of its mental resources in the
process, *all* the team members must be involved. For a team to
continue to develop as a team and ensure that everyone feels fully
included in the team, then *all* members must be involved. Thus,
the third special competency that team coaches require is the ability to help every member of a team participate fully in whatever
the team is doing.

Involvement begins with having team norms that make full participation an explicit expectation. But teams do not always adhere
to their norms. Team members may feel at times that they have
nothing to contribute. Whatever the reason for individuals not staying fully involved in a team's meeting, coaches will need to test
what looks like noninvolvement whenever it occurs. Coaches can
test involvement in several ways.

Questioning Individuals

A coach may question individuals: "What do you think of that,
John?" "Will that idea work with your customers, Sue?" "We've
heard from the people who are responsible for the air conditioners;
what do you people who work on heat pumps think?"

Appealing to a Member's Competence

A coach may appeal to some member's special competence: "Bob, tell us what happened when you surveyed your customers last year?" "Some of you have used that supplier in your other jobs. What do you think about using him now?"

Making a General Statement

A coach may make a general statement to the whole team about the lack of participation: "I have the feeling that some of us aren't very interested in modifying the way we input job orders. I think we need to test just how important the idea is to all of us." "I don't think we have heard from enough team members to make a decision. I really don't know what most of you think about this."

Basics of Problem Solving and Decision Making in Teams

The third set of competencies that team coaches require is an understanding of basic problem solving and decision making as they apply to teams. It is as unnecessary as it is impossible for every team member to know how to use all of the problem solving and decision making tools that are now available in the many publications on team training and quality improvement. But it is necessary for team members who want to help their teams manage and improve the way that they solve problems and make decisions to have a few tools that they can demonstrate to their teams and help their teams to use. Among the most useful tools for solving problems and making decisions are the structured problem-solving process, opportunity analysis, brainstorming, and the nominal group technique.

Structured Problem-Solving Process

Two questions confront teams: (1) how to fix what is broken and (2) how to improve what is not broken. To answer either of these questions, teams must proceed through an orderly and sequential definition of the problem or opportunity and then devise various strategies for solving the problem or taking advantage of the opportunity. The actual steps that teams go through can be conceptualized in a variety of ways, starting with the simple and proceeding to the more complex. A simple five-step process is outlined below that coaches can use to help their teams identify and solve problems or take advantage of opportunities.

1. *Acknowledge that a problem or opportunity exists.* Customer complaints, costs overruns, slips in schedule, and breakdowns in production machines are some of the many *problems* that can be imposed on a team. *Opportunities* to be embraced can include making happy customers even happier, reducing the variance in products more than the required quality limits, or deciding to increase the efficiency and reliability of some work system that is already performing well. The first step is for the team to accept that there is a problem or opportunity.

2. *Collect data.* Next the team must describe the problem or opportunity in quantitative terms. Suppose you were on a team that was responsible for improving a project management training program. You would need data on the following: (a) whether participants were learning what was taught; (b) whether participants were learning what they needed to know; (c) whether participants retained and applied what they learned; and (d) whether they could apply what they knew to improve the performance of their projects.

3. *Identify causes of the problem or opportunity.* Referring again to the example of the project management training program, suppose you discovered that participants were not learning what they needed to know. The next step would be to find out why they were not learning. The team could use many techniques, such as cause-and-effect diagrams or a simple process of "Why?" analysis. Every time a possible cause for not learning was identified, they could simply ask, "Why?" When the answer to that question was identi-

fied, the group would again ask, "Why?" until they identified the root causes.

4. *Identify possible solutions.* Solutions are strategies to solve problems or to improve some aspect of performance. Teams can test the appropriateness of a solution by specifying the payoffs that the solution would produce.

For example, we might propose that a pocket-sized copy of objectives be made for each participant in a workshop and that before and after each session, participants be asked to review the objectives in teams. The expected payoffs are that participants will know what learning is expected; they will be reminded of their responsibility to reach each learning objective; they will reinforce their learning for each objective; and they will develop a set of resources among their colleagues that will further support their learning.

Once the team has verified the payoffs it expects to obtain from its solutions, it can then take action with confidence.

5. *Act, check, modify.* The final step is to put the solutions into action and then check regularly to find out if the anticipated payoffs are being realized.

In the case of the pocket cards with the course objectives, the team would periodically measure learning against the objectives through written tests, interviews, or application of their learning to some problem.

Opportunity Analysis

Opportunity analysis has proven to be a very powerful activity in the teams that I have coached. It consists of the following steps:

1. Review the systems under the team's control, looking for opportunities for improvement.

2. Select one of the systems and identify elements within it that could be targeted for improvement.

3. Use an information developing and decision-making tool, such as brainstorming or the nominal group technique (described below), to decide how to approach the opportunity.

4. Select the methods with the highest potential payoff.

Once the methods are selected for approaching the opportunity, the team could use the problem-solving outline above or a project-planning outline to build an action plan for taking advantage of the opportunity.

Figure 5.1 shows a typical system with opportunities to improve team performance. As shown, team performance is a function of *team development,* that is, the quality of team meetings, internal communication and cooperation, responsiveness, and the like. Team development is an opportunity for improving team performance. One of the first steps that a coach might propose is that the team assess its current levels of development.

Teams also receive *inputs* (services and products) from internal or external *suppliers.* The quality of these services and products can always be improved in such areas as accuracy, cost, useability, reliability, and performance.

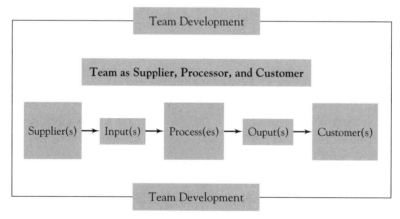

Figure 5.1. General Opportunities for Team Improvement

Work is accomplished in teams, as in any organization, through work *processes*. Work processes can be improved by such actions as eliminating steps, reducing the time it takes to perform steps, eliminating inspections, and improving the consistency in a process's performance.

Teams deliver *outputs* (services and products) to internal or external *customers*. The quality of these services and products can always be improved in such areas as accuracy, cost, useability, reliability, and performance. In addition, the satisfaction of customers can be addressed to measure and improve the perceptions they have of teams' services and products and the expectations they have about these services and products.

The final tools for problem solving and decision making that I will discuss are brainstorming and the nominal group technique. Many people are already familiar with these tools, but they are not always used with the discipline they require. Teams may think they are brainstorming when in fact they are randomly developing and sharing ideas.

Brainstorming

True brainstorming includes the following steps, which must be strictly followed for the best results to be consistently achieved.

1. Clarify ground rules for brainstorming.
2. Define topic or information target.
3. Go around to each member of the group in sequence to request ideas.
4. Record all ideas on a flip chart for everyone to see.
5. After the first few rounds, take input in any order from team members.
6. Follow these rules in generating ideas:

   - State one idea at a time
   - Allow no criticism or discussion

- Record all ideas, even if they seem repetitious
- Piggyback on ideas

7. Review all ideas and clarify, but do not eliminate; reword as needed.

8. Review all ideas and combine ideas that are redundant.

9. Review, clarify, and add in order to develop a final list.

Nominal Group Technique

The nominal group technique has features that brainstorming does not have: (1) it makes it possible for team members to give input anonymously; (2) it provides time for individual preparation before giving input; and (3) it has a built-in weighted voting step for evaluating ideas and making decisions. The steps are described below.

Step 1: Statement of Problem or Objective

The team agrees on a clear definition of the problem or objective of the session and might ask questions such as the following:

- "What opportunities do we have for improving the quality of our services or products?"

- "What problems do we have with the way our team meetings are run?"

- "What team training do we need?"

Step 2: Individual Generation of Ideas

The question or problem statement is displayed so the whole group has a clear view of it. Each team member, working independently, records his or her own responses to the question or problem on an index card, one response per card.

Step 3: Recording and Displaying Ideas

Cards are collected and ideas are recorded on flip charts for the whole team to see. No ideas are rejected, and the exact words from the cards are used.

Step 4: Discussion and Clarification

Next the team discusses, clarifies, combines, and eliminates ideas that are written on the flip chart. All items are reviewed, and obvious duplications are removed. Items are clarified. The potential usefulness of items is not discussed. Only duplicate items are removed from the list. Items are then numbered for easy reference.

Step 5: Preliminary Voting

A preliminary vote is taken on the importance of each idea. The following voting method is used to avoid influence because of status, personality, or pressure to conform. At least three cards are distributed to each member. Members then review the list of ideas and select a number of items equivalent to the number of index cards they have been given. Members then do the following:

1. In the upper left-hand corner of their cards, they write the numbers of the item they have selected (see the illustration below).

```
┌──────────────────────────────────────┐
│ Item                                  │
│ Number                                │
│                                       │
│                                       │
│                                       │
│                                       │
│                                       │
│                                Rank   │
│                                Number │
└──────────────────────────────────────┘
```

2. Team members then review each item they have selected and rank it by writing a number in the lower right-hand corner, with higher numbers being higher rankings. For example, if a team member has five cards, he or she would rank his or her first choice as 5, then second choice as 4, and so on. The item considered least important by that person would have a 1 in the lower right-hand corner.

3. The leader then collects the cards and posts the results. The preliminary vote is discussed to identify any areas of strong disagreement and to ensure that everyone has the same understanding of the results.

Step 6: Final Vote

Teams then repeat the ranking process, using only items that were selected by the members during the first round. A final vote is taken using any number of techniques, if needed, to reduce the list further.

There are many more tools that coaches of teams can well afford to learn. Those described here, however, provide the prospective coach with tools that have immediate and wide application for most teams.

Key Learning Points for Chapter Five

1. Coaching teams, as with coaching one-on-one, is not necessarily an assigned role. Anyone who can help teams solve problems and improve performance can coach the team.

2. To coach a team requires coaches to master the two coaching processes of Responding to Needs and Initiating Alternatives and all the skills that support these processes.

3. Coaching teams requires special knowledge to help teams manage

   • The conditions for effective team meetings

   • Interactions among team members

   • Basic tools for problem solving and decision making

6

. . . .

Self-Development

In the foregoing chapters I have provided the conceptual basis for coaching. Understanding the elements that go into successful coaching is one thing, but actually being a successful coach is another. Successful coaching requires that we have a picture in our heads of what we are doing, for example, following one of the coaching processes described earlier. Coaching, however, is a real-time activity, and what finally makes coaching successful is the quality of the coach's communication. There is only one path to becoming a successful coach and that is to act and be able to evaluate one's actions. Becoming a successful coach requires that we *prepare*, we *practice*, and we *receive feedback* on how well we are doing.

Preparation

Preparation for a coaching session means both general preparation and specific preparation. General preparation includes whatever we might do to improve our performance in all our coaching interactions. Specific preparation includes whatever we might do to be ready for a planned or scheduled coaching interaction.

General Preparation

A lot of coaching will always be unplanned. Some coaching conversations will be brief and some will be extended. Coaching opportunities present themselves whenever a co-worker wants information. Coaching opportunities present themselves any time we give feedback or encourage others. Coaching also occurs under more planned and formal conditions. Whatever the nature of our coaching interactions, all of them are supported by our knowledge of the processes and skills that have been described in the previous chapters. One obvious way to improve our coaching skills is to review periodically the two processes of coaching and the general and specific skills associated with these processes. Here are a few ideas on how to review the processes and skills.

The three stages in Process 1 and Process 2 are easily committed to memory. Process 1 (Involving, Developing, Resolving) is the process that you will use most often. Start with this process, but you can use the same guidelines for reviewing Process 2.

Review the stages and the goals for each stage. It is the goals that give the structure to a coaching interaction. By knowing and being able to describe the stages and goals, you will create a mental structure that will eventually become so familiar that you will find yourself quite unconsciously using the process to structure your coaching interactions.

Once you have the stages of the process well in hand, review the general skills associated with the process. These skills provide the primary support for both Process 1 and Process 2. Try listing the skills by name. Then give the definitions of each skill. Finally, give your own examples of the skills. Repeat this same process for reviewing and learning the stage-specific skills associated with each of the three stages of Process 1.

Another way to make general preparation for all your coaching interactions, especially the extended ones, is to review periodically the examples of coaching interactions that were provided in Chapters Three and Four. Follow the directions for using the examples that accompany them in each chapter.

General preparation increases our skills in managing all our coaching interactions, whenever they may occur. When we have a planned or scheduled coaching conversation, however, we can increase the success of these interactions by making specific preparation.

Specific Preparation

Making specific preparation for a planned coaching conversation may include developing a job aid, rehearsing, or visualizing.

Job Aids

One of the easiest ways to make specific preparation for a scheduled coaching conversation is to keep an outline of the processes handy. This is like using any other job aid to perform a function, such as fixing a lock, procuring supplies, or completing travel documents. By taking time to review the process that is appropriate to the coaching function for which we are planning, we can improve our performance in the following ways:

- Remind ourselves that successful coaching is a process and help us keep in mind the stages of the process that we intend to manage

- Remind ourselves of the goals that we are trying to achieve at each stage, especially the goal of obtaining and strengthening commitment for continuous improvement

- Remind ourselves of the specific kinds of communication skills that we must use to support the coaching process

Rehearsing

Another way to prepare for a planned coaching session is to know exactly what we plan to say. Rehearsing is particularly useful when a coach is preparing for a session to confront poor performance. The coach largely determines how these sessions start, and how they start often determines how successful the rest of the conversation will be. By rehearsing, even writing down, the exact words of the confrontation, the coach will ensure that the confrontation is concrete, limited, and future oriented.

Visualizing

We can also prepare for coaching sessions by imagining what the first few interchanges of the session may sound like. Taking time to develop a mental picture of what might happen during a coaching session has special value in sessions to improve performance. We can picture alternative ways that the person being coached might respond to our initial confrontation or challenge and then practice framing a response that encourages the other person to expand and explore his or her thoughts and concerns. Visualizing is particularly useful when we know that we have a coaching session coming up in which we plan to confront the other person about some performance problem. Imagine the other person responding to our confrontation with words that are very defensive, or aggressive, or passive. What are the words that we imagine the other person saying? What words might we say in response?

Practice

Preparation is one way to develop ourselves as coaches. Another way is to practice the use of the processes and skills of successful coaching in the many conversations that we have with individuals and with teams. We can practice the use of an entire coaching process or we can practice using any of the many skills—especially those identified as general skills for the two processes in Exhibits 3.1 and 4.2.

Every team meeting in which we participate presents us with opportunities to practice the communication skills of coaching. When others speak, we can use skills such as probing and reflecting to encourage them to become clear about what they are saying and to help the entire team understand what is being said.

There are many other opportunities to practice our coaching skills as team members. Opportunities to help the team solve problems and learn new knowledge and skills occur all the time. It is also common that teams must be confronted about a performance problem or urged to take the next step to become an even better team. One easy way to begin to practice our coaching skills with teams is to offer to teach the team some new tool for solving problems, measuring performance, improving customer satisfaction, or improving the performance of a work process. Most teams do not use tools such as statistical process control, value analysis, or other sophisticated tools—all of which could help them improve their performance. Teaching teams to use any of these tools will benefit our teams, plus give us the chance to practice our coaching skills.

In most of our conversations with individuals as well as teams, we can practice all of the general skills identified in the two coaching processes. All of the skills can be practiced by first reviewing what they are, then using them in various situations, and observing the results. For example, take the skill of attending. Once we are clear about the characteristics of good attending, we can practice attending any time we have a conversation—even the most casual. Notice what happens when we face another person and maintain good eye contact. Notice what happens when we do not.

When people talk to us, we can consciously use the skills of acknowledging and reflecting and mentally record what happens. Test using a sequence of closed probes during a conversation and notice any differences in what the other person does when we start using open probes.

Apart from practicing our skills in conversations, we can also practice them by framing responses to written or voiced statements. Here, for example, are a few statements. Imagine that they have been said to you in a conversation. Write out three different responses to each: a closed probe, an open probe, and a reflecting response.

> *Statement 1:* "I have no idea where I'm headed right now. I really don't like what I'm doing, but I don't know what I might do that I would like better."

Closed Probe:

Open Probe:

Reflecting:

> *Statement 2:* "I don't understand how to install a new version of the word processing software when there isn't enough space on my hard drive."

Closed Probe:

Open Probe:

Reflecting:

> *Statement 3:* "How do we keep our team from just taking on the characteristics of the lowest denominator? This consensus stuff doesn't make sense to me in a research environment like ours."

Closed Probe:

Open Probe:

Reflecting:

Another way to practice our general coaching skills is to listen to the many interviews that take place on radio and television and to put ourselves in the place of the person conducting the interview. As we listen to the person being interviewed, we can practice how to use skills such as acknowledging, probing, or reflecting in response.

Feedback

As with every kind of skill development, improving ourselves as coaches requires that we receive feedback on our performance. For feedback to have the highest value for managing our skill development, it must be framed against the most rigorous standards that we can produce. If we receive feedback that only tells us that we demonstrated poor attending skills, that is limited information. If we receive feedback that tells us we were twirling a pencil and maintaining very little eye contact, that sort of information can be used. If we receive feedback that tells us we made a poor confrontation, that is of no value. If we are told that our confrontation was very general and the words we used are repeated to us, that information can be used to improve performance.

At the end of this chapter are two coaching feedback forms (Worksheets 6.1 and 6.2) that can be used to ensure that the information we receive is framed against specific standards. Using these forms tells us what we did and what we did not do in such concrete terms that we can gain a clear picture of just how well we are doing.

We can obtain useful feedback from three sources: (1) from self-observation; (2) from the persons coached; and (3) from a third-party observer. Feedback through self-observation is best obtained through the use of videotaping and feedback.

Feedback Through Self-Observation

The general availability of video recording and playback equipment makes it possible for us to observe our own performance. Video recording and feedback have proven to be the most powerful methods we have for teaching and learning communication skills. In the absence of videotaping capability, audiotaping is a good second choice, although obviously the nonverbals are lost. One way to set up a video recording and replay session is to do the following:

1. Contract with a co-worker or friend to participate with you.

2. Select a coaching process and the function that you want to practice.

3. Review with your colleague the process you are going to practice and the emphasis. For counseling situations, your colleague can present any problem at all. You do not need to know in advance what it is. If you are practicing confrontation, you may want to tell your colleague what the problem or opportunity is. You might also tell your colleague how you might want him or her to respond, for example, aggressively, defensively, or passively.

4. Record your coaching interaction for no more than 10 minutes the first time. You can extend this time as you practice and your skills improve.

5. Stop the tape after you have practiced for the allotted time and rewind.

6. Replay the tape and assess your performance using the Coaching Feedback Form appropriate to the process you are using. (Worksheet 6.1 is for Process 1: Responding to Needs and Worksheet 6.2 is for Process 2: Initiating Alternatives.) You can also ask for feedback from your colleague.

7. Rewind and play the tape again. Based on what you learned from your first trial and your assessment, stop the tape at any point at which you think you could improve your performance.

8. Use what you learn to identify what you need to focus on to improve your coaching skills.

Feedback from Persons Coached

Most of us have an aversion to asking people with whom we live and work to give us feedback. Parents rarely request and receive feedback from their children; consequently they have little or no idea of their effect on their children and have little or no information that they can use to improve their performance as parents. Feedback is not always accurate and it is not always helpful, but the person receiving the feedback is always in control. We don't have to use the feedback we receive, but without feedback we doom ourselves to operate in the dark—without the information we need.

It is always possible for coaches to obtain feedback from the individuals and teams that they coach, and it is always possible that this feedback will be helpful. We will never know, of course, whether feedback could be useful unless we begin to request it.

Coaches can structure the way they receive feedback from the persons being coached in many different ways. The following is a simple way to obtain feedback that creates the minimum of uneasiness or stress:

1. At the end of a coaching session, ask the person being coached to give you some feedback about the conversation you have just completed.

2. Use the Coaching Feedback Form (Worksheet 6.1 or 6.2) and ask the person four or five questions based on the form. Do not ask too many questions. Just focus on the areas you want to work on.

3. End the session by asking the other person to give you any additional information that he or she wants to provide.

4. Use what you learn to identify what you need to focus on to improve your coaching skills.

Feedback from a Third Party

It is really necessary to use a third party for feedback only when you do not use videotaping and replay. Here is a suggested sequence:

1. Obtain the cooperation of two colleagues. During the practice session, have one of your colleagues function as the person being coached and the other colleague as the observer.

2. Review the appropriate Coaching Feedback Form with your colleagues.

3. Select a process and one of its functions that you want to use.

4. Review with the colleague who will be coached the problem or topic that you plan to use. If you have selected to practice Process 1 and the counseling function, your colleague may present any problem at all. If you want to practice confrontation, tell your colleague what the problem is, what his or her work relationship with you is, and how you might want your colleague to respond, for example, aggressively, defensively, or passively.

5. Review the appropriate Coaching Feedback Form with the colleague who is the observer so that he or she knows exactly what to look for and record. Also ask the observer to serve as a timer.

6. Conduct your coaching interaction. At the start, limit your interaction to ten minutes.

7. After ten minutes, have the observer stop the session and use the Coaching Feedback Form to obtain feedback.

8. Use the feedback to identify ways that you can improve your coaching skills.

If you have two colleagues who are interested in improving their own coaching skills, you can use the process outlined above with both people, all three of you taking turns as coach, person coached, and observer. If you also use videotaping and feedback, you can build a very powerful learning activity.

Key Learning Points for Chapter Six

1. Coaching is a real-time activity. What finally makes coaching successful is the quality of the coach's communication.

2. Becoming a successful coach requires us to prepare, practice, and receive feedback on how well we are doing.

3. Among the ways that we can prepare for a coaching session are the following:

   • Make a job aid of the process and keep it available during our coaching sessions
   • Rehearse what we intend to say at the outset of a coaching session
   • Build an image or picture in our minds of how the coaching conversation will go

4. We can practice and improve our skills in several ways:

   • By making responses in writing or mentally to sets of practice statements
   • By consciously using them in our conversations with other persons—even our most casual ones
   • By listening to interviews on radio and television and imagining what we might say as the interviewer

5. We can also improve our skills by using the following:

   • Self-feedback through audiotaping or videotaping our practice coaching sessions
   • Feedback from the persons we may coach
   • Feedback from third-party observers

Worksheet 6.1. Coaching Feedback Form for Process 1:
Responding to Needs

1. How often and/or how well did I use the following problem-solving skills?

Skill	Frequency	Quality/Notes
Attending		
Clarifying		
Acknowledging		
Open Probes		
Closed Probes		
Reflecting		
Self-Disclosure		
Immediacy		
Summarizing		
Resourcing		
Reviewing		
Planning		
Affirming		

2. How well did I communicate respect? How might I improve?

3. How well did I stay focused on the problem? How might I improve?

4. How well did I help the conversation progress to produce a satisfactory result? How might I improve?

5. How well did I maintain a positive relationship? How might I improve?

Worksheet 6.2. Coaching Feedback Form for Process 2:
Initiating Alternatives

Observation	Comments	How Might I Improve?
1. Was the presentation or confrontation concrete and specific?		
2. Was the presentation or confrontation future oriented?		
3. Did I respond directly to the other person's reaction to the challenge or confrontation by (a) dropping my own agenda temporarily and (b) using information development skills?		
4. What specific information development skills did I use?		
5. How well did I keep the process focused on the problem and not on the characteristics of the other person?		
6. How well did I communicate respect?		
7. Did I develop an action plan to resolve the problem and a follow-up plan?		

About the Author

. . . .

Dennis C. Kinlaw, Ed.D, received his doctorate in adult education from The George Washington University. He has master's degrees from Wesley Theological Seminary and Garrett Theological Seminary and a Bachelor of Science degree from Florida Southern College. He has taught graduate courses for The American University, The George Washington University, and Virginia Commonwealth University in management theory and practice, human behavior, group dynamics, interpersonal communication, organizational behavior, learning theory, human resource development, program planning and evaluation, and counseling of adults.

For the past twenty years, Kinlaw has been a consultant to organizations and has conducted management training programs. His clients include The Aerospace Corporation, Bell Atlantic Corporation, the Chesapeake and Potomac Telephone Company, Livermore National Laboratory, Louisville Bank for Cooperatives, NASA Goddard Space Flight Center, NASA Headquarters, NASA Kennedy Space Center, NASA Langley Research Center, the National Institutes of Health, the Health Care Finance Administration, and USBI Rocket Booster Corporation.

He is the author of numerous articles in management and training journals; instruments and monographs published by Development Products and Commonwealth Training Associates Publications; the books *Listening and Communicating Skills: A Facilitator's Package*

(Jossey-Bass/Pfeiffer) and *Developing Superior Work Teams* (Jossey-Bass/Pfeiffer); and the first edition of *Coaching for Commitment* and the accompanying trainer's package.

Kinlaw has also served as a chaplain in the U.S. Navy, as an instructor at Virginia Commonwealth University, and as president of Commonwealth Training Associates and Developmental Products, Inc.